UNITED STATES TRAVEL AND TOURISM INDUSTRY

TOURISM AND HOSPITALITY DEVELOPMENT AND MANAGEMENT

Additional books in this series can be found on Nova's website under the Series tab.

Additional E-books in this series can be found on Nova's website under the E-book tab.

TOURISM AND HOSPITALITY DEVELOPMENT AND MANAGEMENT

UNITED STATES TRAVEL AND TOURISM INDUSTRY

DANIELLE P. MOORE
AND
ALLISON G. DOHERTY
EDITORS

Nova Science Publishers, Inc.
New York

LIBRARY OF CONGRESS CATALOGING-IN-PUBLICATION DATA

United States travel and tourism industry / [editors] Danielle P. Moore and
Allison G. Doherty.
    p. cm. -- (Tourism and hospitality development and management)
  Includes bibliographical references and index.
  ISBN 978-1-61209-111-2 (hardcover : alk. paper)
 1. Tourism--United States--Management. 2. Tourism--United
States--Planning. 3. Hospitality industry--United States. I. Moore,
Danielle P. II. Doherty, Allison G.
 G155.U6U573 2011
 338.4'79173--dc22
                                                                        2010047107

Published by Nova Science Publishers, Inc. † New York

CONTENTS

PREFACE

The U.S. travel and tourism sector, the main economic and employment engine in a number of states, suffered a steep decline in 2008 and 2009 as the nation sank into recession. Though the United States remained the world's top travel destination by dollar value, spending by foreign visitors in the country plunged 15% in 2009. Travel and tourism, which account for 6% of U.S. employment, began to rebound in 2010, but there have been concerns about a possible decline in business along the Gulf Coast due to the April 2010 BP oil spill. This new book examines the U.S. travel and tourism industry today and the challenges and issues for the future

Chapter 1- The U.S. travel and tourism sector, the main economic and employment engine in a number of states, suffered a steep decline in 2008 and 2009 as the nation sank into recession. Though the United States remained the world's top travel destination by dollar value, spending by foreign visitors in the country plunged 15% in 2009—a record. U.S. tourism-related businesses shed nearly 400,000 workers in 2009. The layoffs exceeded the job loss in 2001, when the September 11 terrorism attacks crippled business and pleasure travel. Travel and tourism—which account for 6% of U.S. employment— began to rebound in 2010, but there have been concerns about a possible decline in business along the Gulf Coast due to the April 2010 BP oil spill.

Chapter 2- Real spending on travel and tourism increased at an annual rate of 3.0 percent in 2010:2, following an increase of 5.0 percent (revised) in 2010:1. By comparison, real gross domestic product (GDP) increased 1.6 percent (second estimate) in 2010:2 after increasing 3.7 percent in 2010:1. Travel and tourism prices increased 2.7 percent in 2010:2 after increasing 4.1 percent (revised) in 2010:1.

- Passenger air transportation spending increased 3.9 percent in 2010:2 and 4.0 percent in 2010:1.
- Accommodations spending decelerated, increasing 6.1 percent in 2010:2 after increasing 13.4 percent in 2010:1.
- Prices for accommodations turned up in 2010:2, increasing 19.0 percent, after decreasing 6.4 percent in 2010:1.

Chapter 3- The United States is the number two destination for global international travel.

- International travel and tourism accounts for approximately four percent of total travelers within the United States.
- But where it counts – "total spending, employment, payroll and taxes" - the international travel share is about ten percentage points higher, roughly 14 percent of all U.S. travel.
- International travelers support an estimated 1.1 million jobs and generate about $17 billion in federal, state and local taxes

Chapter 4 - This chapter by the U. S. Department of Commerce highlights the top 10 International Markets of 2009 by both visitation and spending.

Chapter 5- The Department of Commerce's economic accounts data show that the travel and tourism industry generated a record $1.38 trillion in sales for the economy in 2008. The industry directly and indirectly supported more than 8.6 million jobs. From a trade perspective, international travel to the United States represents over one-fourth (26 percent) of all U.S. services exports. In 2008, this translated to $142.1 billion in receipts generated from a record 58 million international visitors. For the 20th consecutive year, travel and tourism produced a travel trade surplus for the United States — a record $29.7 billion — and directly supported more than 900,000 jobs in the United States in 2008.

Chapter 6- Chairman Klobuchar, Ranking Member Martinez and other distinguished Members of the Committee: Thank you for the opportunity and privilege to appear before you on behalf of Carlson Hotels Worldwide and the greater Carlson organization. I would particularly like to thank Senator Klobuchar for your leadership in calling this hearing and your passionate support of the travel industry both in our home state of Minnesota and in the national arena.

Chapter 7- Chairwoman Klobuchar, Senator Martinez, Members of the Committee, my name is Sam Gilliland, and I am Chairman and CEO of Sabre Holdings, the world's largest travel distribution company. Among our businesses are the Sabre global distribution system, which powers corporate and leisure travel agencies, and Travelocity.com, the online travel company that gives consumers the opportunity at any time, day or night, to find and compare amazing travel bargains in the U.S. and around the world. Today, I'll share with you a sampling of these deals that I hope will push Americans out of their nests and back into the air to destinations both here and abroad.

Chapter 8- I appreciate the opportunity to be here today to discuss America's competitive position in travel and tourism—and to explain how increasing foreign travel to the United States can play a vital role in our nation's economic recovery.

I come wearing two hats, both as immediate past Chairman of the U.S. Travel Association--which represents a $740 billion industry employing 7.7 million Americans--and as Chairman of Walt Disney Parks and Resorts, which employs 90,000 people and operates 11 theme parks on three continents, a top-rated cruise line, a major tour wholesaler and more than 34,000 hotel rooms.

The travel industry is vital to our nation's economic health. It generates $2 billion in spending every *day*, and provides $115 billion in tax revenue to the federal, state and local governments. But along with the rest of the economy, the travel industry has suffered during this recession, incurring its share of lost revenue and jobs.

Chapter 9- Good morning Senators and thank you for the invitation to participate in today's hearing. As you are aware, May 9-17 is National Travel and Tourism Week. Yesterday in Las Vegas, hundreds of individuals rallied at the Las Vegas Convention Center in a show of unity and pride for what travel and tourism provides to Southern Nevada. It is the number one industry for Las Vegas. In fact, the travel and tourism industry is the number one economic stimulus for the entire State of Nevada.

Approximately 250,000 people in Las Vegas are employed because of tourism. Three of every 10 jobs in Las Vegas are directly related to travel and tourism. The industry generates more than $30 billion for the local economy ever year. Over the past 50 years, room tax revenue generated by leisure tourists and conventions and meetings delegates has contributed approximately $2 billion to help fund the construction of schools, roads, parks and other local government services.

Chapter 10- It is safe to say that the world is now entering a new golden age for travel and tourism. A confluence of developments is fueling an era of explosive growth in the world travel market – which is likely to drive a sizable share of the world's future job creation, economic growth and tax revenue. Simply put, travel and tourism, which includes leisure, business, conventions and meetings, educational and medical travel, is one of – if not the most – significant growth industries in the world today.

In: United States Travel and Tourism Industry   ISBN: 978-1-61209-111-2
Editors: D.P. Moore and A.G. Doherty   © 2011 Nova Science Publishers, Inc.

Chapter 1

U.S. TRAVEL AND TOURISM INDUSTRY*

Suzanne M. Kirchhoff

SUMMARY

The U.S. travel and tourism sector, the main economic and employment engine in a number of states, suffered a steep decline in 2008 and 2009 as the nation sank into recession. Though the United States remained the world's top travel destination by dollar value, spending by foreign visitors in the country plunged 15% in 2009—a record. U.S. tourism-related businesses shed nearly 400,000 workers in 2009. The layoffs exceeded the job loss in 2001, when the September 11 terrorism attacks crippled business and pleasure travel. Travel and tourism—which account for 6% of U.S. employment—began to rebound in 2010, but there have been concerns about a possible decline in business along the Gulf Coast due to the April 2010 BP oil spill.

Partly in response to the sharp downturn in the sector, Congress passed, and President Obama in March 2010 signed into law, the Travel Promotion Act (P.L. 111-145), creating a nonprofit corporation that will receive up to $100 million annually in federal funds through 2014 to market the United States as an international travel destination. Lawmakers have proposed

---

* This is an edited, reformatted and augmented version of Congressional Research Service publication, Report R41409, dated September 15, 2010.

initiatives to aid Gulf tourism-related businesses affected by the oil spill, and legislation (H.R. 4676) to provide $50 million in government grants over five years for domestic tourism marketing efforts. At the same time, a number of states and localities have increased taxes on tourism-based businesses, including levies on hotel rooms and car rentals. Such efforts are spurring a pushback by consumers and businesses that is spilling into Congress, including a bill (H.R. 4175) to limit the ability of states and localities to impose future taxes on automobile rentals. In addition, the online hotel booking industry is seeking legislation to set a national standard for hotel taxation.

While lawmakers have enacted or proposed specific legislation to aid travel and tourism, most congressional activities that affect the sector, sometimes in a major fashion, are indirect. The sector feels the impact of congressional action on such issues as the minimum wage; funding for national parks, forests, and historical sites; gaming industry regulation; and visa and immigration policy. As travel and tourism have developed from an "invisible" area of the economy—one that businesses and officials considered important, but for which there was little comprehensive data—to a widely analyzed sector, it has become a larger factor in legislative give-and-take in select areas. For example, some lawmakers from states with major coastal tourism businesses oppose proposals to expand offshore oil and gas drilling, based on tradeoffs or perceived tradeoffs between the energy and tourism industries. Likewise, many tourism-related businesses have weighed in on debates regarding homeland security and immigration, asking Congress to streamline the process for obtaining a visa to visit the United States or to go through airport security, arguing that current policies serve as a deterrent to would-be visitors.

TRAVEL AND TOURISM: AN ECONOMIC DRIVER

The travel and tourism sector—transportation, lodging, entertainment, meals and associated products used during journeys for business and pleasure—is a significant component of the U.S. and world economy. According to the United Nations World Tourism Organization (UNWTO), tourism has expanded in the post-World War II-era to become one of the world's largest export industries and the largest global source of foreign exchange earnings for many developing nations.[1]

The number of international tourist trips rose from 25 million in 1950 to an estimated 806 million in 2005, for an annual average growth rate of 6.5%.[2] The figure is projected to reach 1.6 billion by 2020.[3] "The substantial growth of the tourism activity clearly marks tourism as one of the most remarkable economic and social phenomena of the past century," the UNWTO says.

In the United States, about 8.1 million Americans now work in what the U.S. Department of Commerce has defined as travel- and tourism-related businesses including restaurants, hotels, the airlines and the gaming industry.[4] (See Appendix C for complete listing.) The travel and tourism sector accounted for 6% of domestic employment in early 2010 and about a quarter of U.S. services exports.[5] Business trips, which the U.S. Department of Commerce counts as a component of the sector, are a third of travel and tourism activity.[6]

While the United States has the world's largest tourism industry, by dollar value,[7] travel and tourism experienced a sharp year-over-year decline in 2009, due mainly to the recession that began in December 2007. U.S. tourism exports (the amount of money that foreign visitors spend in the United States) plunged by 15% in 2009 from the previous year—a record.[8] Travel and tourism-related businesses shed a record 4.6% of jobs, or 392,000 positions in 2009. That compares to the 128,000 jobs (1.5%) lost in 2001 and 284,000 (3.4%) jobs lost in 2002, when the sector experienced a major contraction after the September 11, 2001 terrorism attacks.[9] Though the sector has begun to rebound, there is concern about potential job and financial loss in tourism-related businesses on the U.S. Gulf Coast as a result of the April 2010 BP oil spill.

Partly in response to the steep downturn in the sector, Congress passed, and President Obama in March 2010, signed legislation (P.L. 111-145) creating the nonprofit Corporation for Travel Promotion, which will receive federal funding of up to $100 million annually to market the United States as an international destination, with matching contributions from industry. During the 111th Congress, lawmakers have also introduced bills to reduce the tax burden on Gulf Coast tourism-related affected by the BP oil spill, and to authorize $50 million in grants over five years to promote tourism in different regions of the country (H.R. 4676). In July 2010 President Obama signed the Cruise Vessel Safety and Security Act (P.L. 111-207) spelling out safety procedures and consumer protections for cruise ships. Lawmakers are also debating measures that could crimp the ability of states and localities to tax tourists, including H.R. 4175, which seeks to limit future state and local taxes on automobile rentals. The online travel booking industry has pushed for national standards that could pre-empt state and local policies on taxation of hotel rooms.[10]

Though lawmakers have taken or proposed specific steps to aid the tourism industry, most of Congress's activities in regard to the sector, while crucially important in many cases, are far more indirect. The sector, which is a major employer in many states and the main economic driver in a number of regions, is affected by congressional action on such issues as the minimum wage; federal funding for national parks, forests and historical sites; gaming industry regulation; and visa and immigration policy. As travel and tourism have developed from an "invisible" area of the economy—one that businesses and officials considered important, but for which there was little comprehensive data—to a widely analyzed sector, it become a larger factor in legislative give- and-take on some issues. For example, some lawmakers from states with major coastal tourism businesses oppose proposals to expand offshore oil and gas drilling, based on tradeoffs or perceived tradeoffs between the energy and tourism industries.[11] Likewise, many tourism-related businesses have weighed in on debates regarding homeland security and immigration, asking Congress to streamline the process for obtaining a visa to visit the United States or go through airport security, arguing that current policies serve as a deterrent to would-be visitors.[12]

GROWTH OF THE TOURISM INDUSTRY

People have long engaged in tourism, including the ancient Greeks who journeyed to the Olympic Games (which even a millennia ago were a mix of athletic competition and business promotion).[13] The modern tourism sector began to take shape in the 19th century as steamboats and passenger trains improved the ease and speed of travel. One prominent company, Cook's Tours, helped shape the industry by offering pre-packaged Grand Tour excursions through Europe and beyond, starting in the mid-1800s.[14]

The number of Americans traveling overseas rose at an annual rate of about 5% per year from 1820 to 2000. While that growth was largely supported by the nation's expanding economy and population, it far exceeded the enlargement of both.[15] In the mid 1800s, the bulk of American travelers venturing abroad were traveling for pleasure or dual purpose of business and tourism.[16] Social legislation in a number of countries in the late 19th and early

20th century that guaranteed paid holidays or time played a role in the evolution the industry.[17]

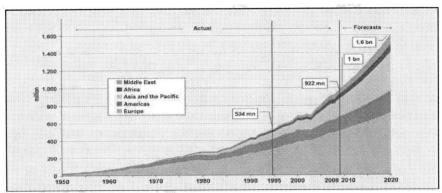

Source: United Nations World Trade Organization, *Tourism Highlights,* 2009 Edition.

Figure 1. International Tourist Arrivals, 1950-2020

The post-World War II expansion of the sector has been driven, among other things, by rising affluence, the growing availability of the automobile, the advent of low-cost air travel, electronic reservation systems and state-funded tourism promotion and infrastructure. Business travel now accounts for a third of the U.S. domestic market.[18] Taxpayer-funded conference and convention centers around the country, for example, compete with each other to host trade shows, conventions and other business gatherings.[19]

DEFINING AND MEASURING THE TOURISM SECTOR

The travel and tourism sector is diffuse and tricky to define. The U.S. Department of Commerce has long had a comprehensive system for measuring domestic economic output. The system works reasonably well in estimating the size of industries like manufacturing—counting the number of widgets produced in a factory, for example, and the number of people working in the widget plant. But travel and tourism as a whole do not fit neatly into the Commerce regime. Tourism is not one industry, but a measure of consumption across a range of industries. Travelers buy goods and services such as performance tickets, airline fares, restaurant meals and hotel or other accommodations manufactured or delivered by a variety of firms.[20] The sector is geographically dispersed and includes public expenditures on such things as state marketing and promotion efforts and transportation systems. A further complication is the fact that the same family of products is often consumed by both tourists and individuals who are not traveling. A Miami retailer may sell sunscreen to a vacationing Midwestern family, as well as to a local resident who applies it before mowing his yard.

To address these difficulties the UNWTO, beginning in the mid-1990s, spearheaded an international push to create a broad, consistent gauge of travel and tourism. Partly as a result of the effort, and a 1995 White House Conference on Travel and Tourism that included a call for more comprehensive information on the sector, the United States is among many countries now using a measurement system known as Tourism Satellite Accounts (TSAs).[21] The U.S. version of the system generally complies with UNWTO standards, though it is not as detailed as is the case in some other nations where tourism constitutes a larger share of economic activity.

The U.S. Department of Commerce Bureau of Economic Analysis (BEA), beginning with prototype accounts based on 1992 data, now compiles annual and quarterly data on tourism spending through Travel and Tourism Satellite Accounts (TTSAs). The TTSAs are designed to capture the broad range of spending by "visitors"—people who travel away from home for less than a year, to places and for purposes outside of normal activities, including trips for business, religious or educational activities.[22] Visitors include residents and international visitors traveling in the United States, as well as U.S. residents traveling out of the country.[23]

The TTSA definition of "visitor" encompasses activities that may not comport with what people generally think of as tourism, or travel for pleasure. But the definition allows for a broad look at travel and tourism as an economic sector, including broad funding flows and supply-demand balances for related businesses, such as hotels and restaurants.[24] As one analysis noted, "While it might seem straightforward to distinguish business from leisure travel, in practice it is not always clear what the visitor actually did. The boundary between travel for leisure and that for personal or family reasons is even more vague."[25]

To estimate the economic impact of travel and tourism, the BEA has identified 24 types of goods and services that are generally purchased by visitors, in the broad areas of lodging, food and beverage services, transportation and recreation.[26] Transportation is the largest component of travel and tourism spending. (See **Appendix A** for full listing.)

The BEA uses a variety of data—production and trade statistics, consumer surveys, employment information, and other sources—to estimate the share of the selected goods and services consumed by visitors during their journeys. For example, the BEA assumes that about 20% of U.S. restaurant meals are purchased by visitors, along with 100% of hotel rooms and about 25% of taxi trips.[27]

The BEA looks at direct spending, which is goods and services bought by travelers, and indirect spending, which is economic activity related to the production of goods, such as plastic for souvenir key chains or shampoo and conditioner provided in hotel bathrooms.

Table 1. Total Tourism-Related Output
(Millions of Dollars)

	2006	2007	2008	2009
Traveler accommodations	$191,675	$207,075	$210,793	$184,499
Transportation	$473,728	$495,580	$520,699	$445,851
Passenger air transportation	$178,276	$185,234	$189,207	$158,517
All other transportation-related commodities	$295,487	$310,395	$331,596	$287,457
Food services and drinking places	$221,780	$232,056	$241,247	$243,351
Recreation, entertainment, and shopping	$364,240	$372,574	$379,644	$378,679
Recreation and entertainment	$135,846	$140,294	$140,583	$140,599
Shopping	$228,395	$232,290	$239,054	$238,076
All tourism goods and services	$1,251,382	$1,307,275	$1,352,316	$1,252,392
Percent change at annual rate	7.5%	4.5%	3.4%	-7.4%

Source: U.S. Department of Commerce, Bureau of Economic Analysis, Travel and
    Tourism Satellite Accounts.
Notes: Output is a measure akin to sales of goods and services, with adjustments for
    changes in inventory, the cost of inputs and other factors. It includes international
    and domestic travel.

Based on the TTSAs, the BEA estimates that tourism-related economic activity was $1 .252 trillion in 2009. Travel and tourism's estimated share of GDP is larger than that of many industries such as utilities, computer and electronic products manufacturing or broadcasting and telecommunications.[28] The travel and tourism sector slowed significantly in 2009, however, mainly in response to the recession that began in 2007. (See Table 1.)

The TTSAs provide a consistent measure over time, and enable analysts to compare the U.S. travel and tourism sector to other industries and other nations that use similar methodology. There is currently no agreed upon system, however, for creating state or local satellite accounts, though some private forecasting firms have developed similar products. Due to measurement difficulties, the national TTSAs exclude certain, relevant items such as vacation home rentals, which means they may understate the size of the travel and tourism sector, according to the BEA.

For example, the BEA includes spending on rental cars in the accounts, but does not calculate the impact of consumer-owned or -leased vehicles, though by some measures more than 90% of leisure trips are made in personal cars. The BEA in a 2007 article estimated that adding data on such automobiles would have boosted the size of the tourism industry as measured by the TTSAs by more than $50 billion in 1998.[29] In addition, the UNWTO has launched a project to develop methods for measuring the meetings sector, which is becoming a more significant part of tourism spending.[30]

Imports and Exports

Another key tourism indicator is imports and exports. Tourism exports refers to money spent by foreign visitors in the United States, while imports refers to money spent by U.S. residents traveling abroad. Spending by international visitors to the United States is watched closely by businesses because overseas visitors tend to take longer trips than domestic tourists and spend far more during their journeys.[31] International travelers made up 4% of total travelers in 2009, but represented 17% of travel-related spending, including 21% of lodging spending, and 15% of food and beverage sales.

The United States has the world's largest tourism sector, in dollar terms, and is the second most popular destination for world travelers, after France.[32] In 2009, the United States had a positive $21.9 billion trade surplus in travel and tourism spending, meaning foreign visitors spent more here than U.S. tourists spent abroad.[33] Roughly 55 million foreign visitors traveled to the United States in 2009, though that figure was down by 3 million from 2008. (See Appendix B for a listing of top foreign markets.)

Not only did fewer international tourists visit the United States in 2009, their spending dropped to $121 billion from the 2008 total of $142 billion—a record decline.[34] The plunge followed strong growth in spending by foreign tourists from 2004 to 2008. (See Figure 2.)

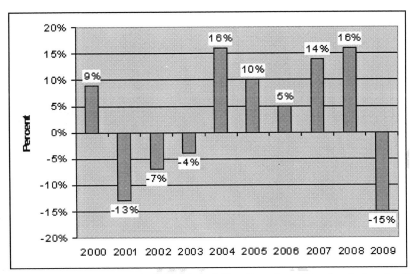

Source: International Trade Administration, Office Travel and Tourism Industries, *U.S. Travel and Tourism Industries: A Year in Review: 2009.*
Notes: Travel exports refers to international visitor spending in the United States.

Figure 2. Changes in U.S. Travel and Tourism Exports Annual Percentage Change in Foreign Visitor Spending

Groups such as the U.S. Travel Association, which represents the domestic travel industry, note that the number of overseas visitors to the United States in 2009 was below the levels prior to the September 11, 2001 terrorist attacks. The organization has pressed for policies to streamline the process for awarding U.S. visas to foreign travelers, saying that in some nations citizens must travel prohibitively long distances to obtain visas.[35] A provision in S. 3676, the FY20 11 Department of State, Foreign Operations, and Related Programs Appropriations Act, would create a pilot program allowing visa interviews to be conducted via secure videoconferencing, rather than in person.

Conventional wisdom is that the terrorist attacks on September 11, 2001, prompted a substantive change in U.S. immigration policy on visa issuances and the grounds for excluding foreign nationals from the United States.

However, a series of laws enacted in the 1990s, however, may have done as much or more to set current U.S. visa policy and the legal grounds for exclusion.[36]

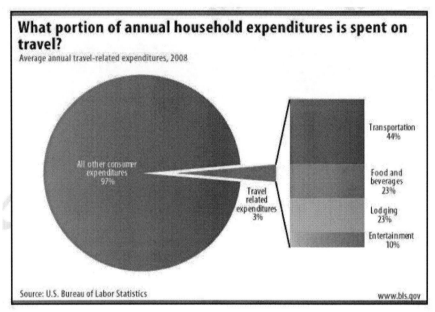

What portion of annual household expenditures is spent on travel?
Average annual travel-related expenditures, 2008

All other consumer expenditures 97%

Travel related expenditures 3%

Transportation 44%

Food and beverages 23%

Lodging 23%

Entertainment 10%

Source: U.S. Bureau of Labor Statistics   www.bls.gov

Source: U.S. Department of Labor, Bureau of Labor Statistics, *Spotlight on Travel.*

Figure 3. Annual U.S. Household Spending on Leisure Travel

Household Spending

In addition to other data on travel and tourism, the U.S. Department of Labor compiles survey- based information on travel-related spending by households. In 2008, the most recent year for which figures are available, U.S. households spent an average of $1,415 on transportation, lodging, food and beverages, and entertainment while on trips for pleasure. The figure represented 3% of all U.S. household spending. (See Figure 3.)

The top 20% of American households in terms of income (those with pretax income of $93,000 or more a year) spend more on travel annually than the combined total of all other U.S. households.[37] Though travel and tourism have become more widespread in recent decades, well- off Americans are still far more likely to travel that those with lesser income.

Employment

The federal government and many states produce estimates of travel and tourism employment. The TTSAs generate figures for sector-wide, direct employment (hotel staff, tour guides) and indirect tourism employment (e.g., people working for companies that make souvenirs that are later sold to tourists). Overall, according to the TTSA calculations, 8.1 million people worked in tourism-related businesses in the first quarter of 2010.[38] Of that total 5.6 million, or 69%, were in direct tourism jobs, with the remaining 2.5 million in indirect tourism areas.[39] (See Appendix C.) Tourism-related employment has declined from a peak of more than 8.6 million jobs in 2007, with the vast bulk of the job loss in 2009, when about 400,000 jobs disappeared. The 8.1 million people who work in travel and tourism represented about 6% of U.S. employment at the end of the first quarter of 2010.[40]

The World Travel & Tourism Council (WTTC), an organization of businesses and government officials, estimates that tourism generates about 8% of all jobs worldwide. In a recent forecast, the WTTC predicted tourism's share of global employment could reach 9.2% by 2020.[41]

Table 2. U.S. Travel-Related Employment and Wages, by Select Occupation Data for Calendar Year 2009

Occupation	Mean Annual Wage	Employment
Hotel, motel, and resort desk clerks	$21,130	224,360
Reservation and transportation ticket agents and travel clerks	$32,400	142,500
Flight attendants	$43,350	95,810
Travel agents	$32,450	76,990
Lodging managers	$53,500	31,660
Tour guides and escorts	$25,990	31,630
Travel guides	$33,300	4,270

Source: U.S. Department of Labor, Bureau of Labor Statistics, *Spotlight on Travel*.
Note: Average earnings for all U.S. occupations were $43,460 in 2009.

U.S. Department of Labor data on employment and wages in some travel-related industries, a subset of the overall sector, indicate that many types of U.S. travel and tourism jobs pay less on average than the nation's mean wage of $43,460. (See Table 2.)[42] According to the U.S. Department of Labor, for example, the average wage for waiters and waitresses in 2009 was $17,670, while maids and housekeepers averaged $19,250.[43] An estimated 4 million people employed in the travel and tourism sector work in hotels and restaurants. (See Appendix C.)

The lower wage levels may reflect the fact that many travel-and-tourism-related jobs are seasonal or part time and require fewer skills than other occupations. Turnover in travel- and entertainment-related businesses tends to be higher than for the labor force as a whole.

TYPES OF TOURISM

Tourism encompasses a wide range of activities, from hiking in the Adirondacks to gambling in Las Vegas, to attending a business meeting in Des Moines. Thousands of companies nationwide arrange tour packages, book hotel rooms, and arrange meetings and other special events. As consumer preferences have evolved, so has the industry. Some leading, or rapidly developing, areas of tourism include the following:

Sport Tourism. Travel to watch or participate in sporting events is one of the fastest-growing areas of the global travel and tourism industry. Some analysts predict sport-related tourism will make up more than 10% of the international tourism spending by the end of 201 0.[44] Major events include the Winter and Summer Olympics, the World Cup and the Super Bowl. Many lesser- known events are important parts of sport tourism, such as high school softball tournaments or speedway racing. For example, the Alabama Gulf Coast Sports Commission says sports-related tourism spending through the first seven months of 2010 was $10.4 million, outpacing the total for all of 2009. Baseball and softball tournaments in the region were an important growth driver.[45]

Heritage Tourism. This form of tourism is generally defined as travel "to experience the places and activities that authentically represent the stories and people of the past and present."[46] During the past 25 years, Congress has established 49 National Heritage Areas in the United States to commemorate, conserve and promote natural, scenic, historic, cultural and recreational resources.[47] The federal Bureau of Land Management, for example, has held workshops and produced educational activities on heritage tourism, recognizing that it is a growing activity on federal lands.[48]

Sustainable or ecotourism. Sustainable tourism describes activities that take advantage of natural resources or other natural attributes, but which are designed to minimize environmental impacts. The George Washington University and the International Ecotourism Society (TIES) jointly offer online courses in sustainable tourism management.[49] Ecotourism is often carried out and promoted via public-private partnerships.[50] A number of organizations inspect and verify that hotels and other facilities that bill themselves as eco friendly meet certain standards. Among groups active in the sector are greenglobe.org, established by the WTTC, and blueflag.org, a Danish organization that verifies whether eco friendly beaches and marinas are indeed that.

Meetings/Conventions. Business travel makes up a third of travel and tourism. Major business hubs like New York City or Los Angeles attract a large volume of business travel. But other areas actively compete for such travelers via marketing and by building and financing large convention centers and hotels. The amount of exhibit space in the United States and Canada, including convention facilities that are either publicly funded or affiliated with private hotels, for example, has doubled since the 1970s, by one estimate.[51] (See "Tourism-Dependent Industries.")

Medical Tourism. Travel to another country or region to access medical services that are more expensive or are unavailable near a consumer's home is known as medical tourism. In the United States, a number of companies specialize in linking prospective patients with overseas doctors and hospitals. A nonprofit group, the Medical Tourism Association, represents health care providers, insurers and travel facilitators in the United States and other countries.[52] Some organizations focus on domestic medical tourism, helping patients compare hospitals around the country.[53] Survey data suggest that up to 2 million Americans went overseas for health care in 2008, with forecasts that the number could rise to 6 million by 2010.[54]

Agritourism. A number of rural areas try to supplement income from farming and natural resource activities by creating or expanding tourism-related businesses. According to the Virginia Cooperative Extension Service: "Agricultural tourism allows farm operators to increase income through a variety of service initiatives such as farm demonstrations, harvest festivals, farm vacations, school group tours, hay rides, pick-your-own crop harvests, bed and breakfasts, campgrounds, crop mazes and a host of other products and services."[55] The University of California San Diego, based on a 2009 survey of 554 California farmers, estimated that more than 2.4 million visitors traveled to that state's farms and ranches in 2008, many of them on day trips. Of the farms surveyed, 12% reported 20,000 or more visitors during the year. The survey noted that California wineries are particularly efficient tourism destinations, attracting a large number of visitors.[56]

TOURISM GEOGRAPHY

Travel and tourism have advanced from a pastime mainly accessible to a small slice of the affluent to a mass activity. The United Nations predicts international tourist arrivals alone will reach 1.6 billion by 2020. (See Figure 1.) U.S. tourism is part of that pattern:

> Before 1900, overseas travel was clearly and predominantly done by the elite of American society, and largely by men. Over time, there was an increase in the number of women who went abroad, rising from 10% of travelers in the early 19th century to over half after World War II and possibly before. Perhaps an even more fundamental change was the increase in middle income travelers. The industry rose from one that catered to the elite of American society in the 19th century to what some have described unfavorably as mass tourism.[57]

Governments around the globe now focus on tourism as an economic development strategy, given the popularization and relative ease of travel and more comparable data regarding the economics of the industry, including tourism satellite accounts. The United Nations has identified tourism development as a tool to help alleviate global poverty.[58] Women make up 60% to 70% of the international tourism workforce, which can have a large impact in poor countries with fewer opportunities for women to work.[59]

In the United States, the travel and tourism industry is a major employer in more than half the 50 states, according to the U.S. Travel and Tourism Board, an advisory committee of the Department of Commerce. States routinely operate offices of travel and tourism that provide consumer information, market local travel and tourism destinations, and often provide funding for tourism including improvements, tax incentives, public parks or historic sites, and convention centers.

Travel and tourism reach into every state and region, but they are more important in some areas than in others. (See Table 3.) For example:

- New York City is the nation's top tourist destination, hosting 45 million visitors in 2009, with a goal of 50 million annual visitors by 2012. New York City officials estimate that 311,000 people work in the city's leisure and hospitality industry, with many of those jobs tied to tourism. [60]

- Tourism is the largest industry in Florida, which has an estimated 80 million visitors annually, generating $60 billion in taxable sales revenue.[61]

- Visitors are projected to spend $10.8 billion in Hawaii in 2010. The real state's gross domestic product for the year is forecast at $50 billion.[62]

- In Nevada, taxes on casinos account for about a third of the state's general fund. Las Vegas hosted 36.4 million visitors in 2009.[63]

According to the U.S. Department of Commerce, New York state was the most popular state destination for overseas visitors to the United States in 2009, attracting 33.7% of all foreign visitors. Other states in the top 10 include Florida with 22.2% of visitors, followed by California with 19.5%, Nevada with 8%, Hawaii with 7.8%, Massachusetts with 5.3%, Illinois with 4.9%, Guam with 4.8%, New Jersey with 3.9%, and Texas with 3.8%.[64]

Most Americans are familiar with iconic tourist destinations such as Disney World, Cape Cod or Yosemite National Park, but travel and tourism activity has a large impact in many lesser-known areas. According to one analysis, Colorado and Wyoming are among the top ten states in terms of the number the concentration of jobs tied to travel- and tourism-related businesses.[65] The Federal Reserve Bank of New York in a 2004 paper noted that travel- and tourism-related businesses accounted for 4.1% of overall jobs in the United States in 2001, but were the source of 6.2% of jobs in parts of upstate New York.[66]

Some cities are more dependent than others on tourism for a number of reasons including the fact that they may have a smaller job market or their economic base may not be highly diversified. For example, while Table 3 shows that New York City attracts more visitor spending than other top U.S. destinations, a smaller share of the city's jobs are tied to tourism that other top locales. Honolulu reaps fewer tourist dollars than New York, but more of its jobs are tied to spending by visitors.

One question that has arisen as a number of states face budget pressures is whether governments get an adequate return on investment for tax dollars spent on tourism promotion. A study by independent economic research firm Global Insight examined the decision of the state of Colorado to stop tourism marketing activities between 1993 to 1997. Global Insight found that leisure visits to the state declined by 8.4% from 1994-1997, which was nearly twice the rate of decline as in other states identified as Colorado's competitors for visitors. After Colorado reinstated promotional activities in 1998, its numbers started to rebound.[67]

Table 3. Top 20 U.S. Tourism

Cities	2008 Tourism Spending Index (1)	2008 Tourism Job Concentration Index (2)
New York City	6.33	0.4
Orlando	5.66	3.1
Las Vegas	5.32	2.2
Los Angeles	3.47	0.4
Chicago	2.60	0.4
San Francisco	2.38	0.8
Washington	2.27	0.5
Miami	2.19	1.3
San Diego	2.13	0.9
Atlanta	1.83	0.5
Phoenix	1.59	0.6
Tampa	1.50	0.9
Dallas	1.44	0.4
Boston	1.40	0.6
Houston	1.33	0.2
Honolulu	1.32	1.9
Santa Ana	1.31	0.4
Seattle	1.16	0.4
Philadelphia	1.12	0.4
Minneapolis	1.00	0.4

Source: Global Insight and D.K. Shifflet & Associates.

Notes: (1)The spending index is based on domestic and international tourism spending. The twentieth city = 1 on the scale. The higher the number, the more tourism dollars are spent in the city. (2) This is a measure of tourism jobs as a percentage of total citywide employment. Job concentration may be lower in cities with a large, varied job base.

Other analysts note that taxes assessed for tourism are levied on many firms that may not benefit from the industry, and impose an opportunity cost in terms of reducing the amount of tax revenues available for other services.[68] Dave Marcouiller of the University of Wisconsin- Madison, who has done extensive work on the tourism industry, argues for an approach that goes beyond what he calls "boosterism" to stimulate tourism, to using more integrated planning that looks at the potential economic and cultural impacts of increased tourism.[69]

Congress in the past has voted to fund programs advertising the United States as a tourist destination, only to subsequently pull back from such efforts. Some research has indicated that it is difficult to measure the effectiveness of federal advertising.[70] Most recently, Congress passed and President Obama signed legislation (P.L. 111-145) to create a public-private 11-member board, Corporation for Travel Promotion, to market the United States as a travel destination to overseas visitors. The effort will be funded via a $14 assessment on international visitors from countries that have reciprocal travel agreements with the United States wherein visas are not required for travel, and a matching assessment on the U.S. domestic industry. The government will draw on the fees to provide up to $100 million a year, through 2014, when the act sunsets.[71]

TOURISM AS A DEVELOPMENT TOOL

In the United States, travel and tourism-related industries grew faster than the overall economy on average from the mid-1950s through the 1990s, according to one analysis.[72] Domestic tourism- related spending continued to rise during recessions in the 1950s and 1960s, and during the 1990- 91 downturn.[73] Those trends did not hold up, however, during the 2002 downturn and the deep recession that began in December 2007. The tourism sector took a larger hit than the overall economy in 2009 in terms of percentage of job loss and falloff in overall output.[74] Travel and tourist inflation-adjusted output fell 3.9% in 2009, compared to a 3.7% drop for the U.S. economy as a whole, while 4.6% of jobs in the sector were lost, compared to a 4.3% drop in overall U.S. employment.

Globally, the UNWTO says that in years when world economic growth is more than 4%, tourism tends to expand even faster. When world output falls below 2%, tourism declines by an even larger amount.[75]

The sector is also characterized by volatility stemming from unexpected events or shocks separate from broader economic trends. Adverse weather (too little snow, too much rain), for example, can crimp bookings at resort areas. Environmental disasters such as oil spills can take a toll (see "Gulf Coast Tourism.") Bad publicity or political decisions can sometimes have an impact. Citizen groups, labor unions and other organizations have proposed tourism boycotts in response to policies they disagree with, as is the case with Arizona's recent immigration law.[76]

In another example, some industry officials contend that negative media attention generated by insurance giant American International Group's planned 2008 corporate retreat at an expensive hotel—which came close on the heels of the Federal Reserve's decision to provide emergency aid to the company—prompted other, unrelated firms to curtail business travel.[77] Colliers PFK Consulting, which carries out an annual survey of the industry, says operating income for conference centers declined 43.5% in 2009 from the previous year as business fell off.[78] "During economic recessions it is not uncommon to see associations and corporations cut their meetings budget. However, never before have we seen the stigma attached to organizations that attempted to hold valuable training and planning conferences."[79]

Tourism Pros and Cons

Travel and tourism have become an enticing economic development strategy for a number of states, localities, and countries. On the plus side, the sector is labor-intensive, meaning jobs can be created relatively quickly. Businesses such as guided tours or souvenir shops do not require as much capital or training as manufacturing or technical companies. Tourism-generated spending and special taxes on visitors are a source of external revenue and, politically, may have the added attraction for state and local officials of replacing or reducing the need to impose taxes on residents. Examples include taxes on hotel rooms and automobile rentals. Infrastructure enhancements aimed at attracting tourists, such as new roads built primarily for travelers, better meeting facilities or public-privately funded resort or hotel facilities, may make a region more attractive to local residents as well as other, non-tourism related businesses. According to a look at the pluses and minuses of tourism by Federal Reserve Bank of New York: "Tourism benefits local residents, who enjoy the same cultural amenities as visitors do—such as nightlife, parks and museums, with the added advantage of having these amenities subsidized by nonresidents."[80]

There are also downsides to tourism development. Many tourism-related jobs are seasonal or low-wage. Travel-related businesses such as hotels or restaurants may be owned by national or regional companies that export their profits out of the town or state where they are sited. Local residents may be crowded out of the housing market if an influx of visitors pushes up real estate prices. Over time, overbuilding and overcrowding can put a strain on the natural resources or other attractions that initially lured tourists to a region.[81] States or localities may spend millions of dollars on infrastructure improvements aimed at tourists that do not produce hoped-for benefits. For example, the state of Nevada recently defaulted on municipal bonds used to build a Las Vegas monorail for tourists, which did not spur expected traffic or fares.[82] Local residents may have mixed feelings about tourism. Some research indicates that even when residents welcome the possible economic benefits of tourism, they worry it may create social divides by attracting affluent visitors into an area, but creating lower-paid jobs.[83] Environmental factors are becoming a larger issue, including concerns about the cruise ship industry.[84]

In a broad study examining tradeoffs related to tourism, U.S. Department of Agriculture economists in 2005 looked at 311 rural counties that they defined as "recreation counties" based on such data as the number of entertainment and recreation facilities and real estate market characteristics. The researchers found that the recreation counties had average population growth of 20% during the 1990s, a rate three times as fast as that of other rural counties.[85] Job growth in the recreation counties was more than double that of the other rural areas. Additional benefits included rising land prices, less poverty, higher incomes and more economic diversification. Though housing rental and purchase prices rose, wages tended to rise fast enough to compensate for the higher costs. "While other types of growth can have similar benefits, rural recreation and tourism development may provided greater diversification, and, for many places, it may be easier to achieve than other kinds of development—such as high-tech development—because it does not require a highly educated workforce."[86]

The study noted large differences even among the 311 counties, however. Areas with ski resorts had the healthiest and wealthiest populations. Counties that depended on casino revenue boosted employment and earnings, but also experienced more crime than other counties.[87]

In one example of the tradeoffs and challenges in a tourism-based economy, the Lake Tahoe basin area has long depended on tourism and gaming as the mainstay of its local economy. But the local gaming industry has shed 7,000 jobs since 1990, helping to lead to 15% decline in the area's population between 2000 and 2008.[88] High unemployment in the region, and the fact that 68% of local houses are second homes owned by seasonal visitors, has helped to create a shortage of affordable housing. Consulting firm Applied Development Economics, in a study prepared for a regional consortium looking for ways to retool the Lake Tahoe Basin economy, does not call for abandoning tourism, but de-emphasizing gambling-related tourism and emphasizing areas such as ecotourism, redevelopment using green building and other technologies and a possible emphasis on medical tourism.[89]

Tourism-Dependent Industries

Some U.S. businesses are heavily reliant on travel and tourism, including the lodging sector and the airline industry. The U.S. Commerce Department estimates that 1.6 million U.S. jobs in the hotels, motels and other lodging are tied to travel and tourism, along with 801,000 jobs in the airline sector.[90] These businesses have been hurt by a recent business in both business and leisure travel since 2007. Business-related travel is a third of the domestic travel and tourism industry. (See Figure 4.)

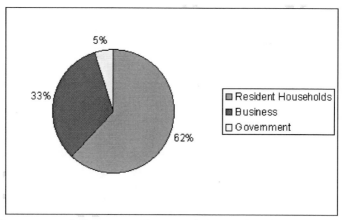

Source: Department of Commerce, Bureau of Economic Affairs, *U.S. Travel and Tourism Satellite Accounts for 2005-2008*, Table J.

Figure 4. 2007 Domestic Travel and Tourism by Category Business travel makes up a third of tourism spending

Business and leisure travel has declined significantly in the United States and worldwide since the recession began in December 2007. The slowdown, along with fluctuating energy and currency prices, problems of overcapacity and other issues, has made the past several years challenging for tourism-dependent industries. Airlines and hotels cut prices sharply from 2008-2009 in an effort to hold on to customers. In recent months they have had begun to reverse those cuts in air fares and room rates. (See Figure 5.)

Airlines

The U.S. airline industry had a net loss of $23.7 billion in 2008, followed by a $2.5 billion decline in 2009. Adding to the industry's woes, energy prices spiked in the summer of 2009, even as airlines were under pressure to reduce fares to attract passengers. (See Figure 5.) The industry has responded to the downturn in travel and tourism by reducing capacity; instituting new fees, such as fees per checked bag; and eliminating some routes. Airlines have also laid off workers. Airline employment had declined for 24 consecutive months, as of June 2010, according to the U.S. Department of Transportation.[91] According to the Air Transport Association, passenger traffic fell in every month of 2009 except September and November.[92]

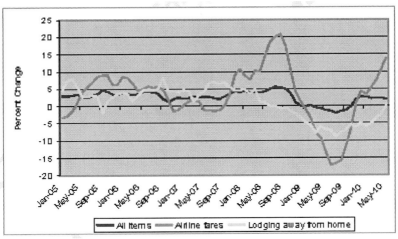

Source: U.S. Department of Labor, Consumer Price Index. Notes: Year-Over-Year Percentage Change.

Figure 5. Airline and Hotel Inflation Fluctuations Airline and hotel prices declined faster than overall inflation in 2009

Airlines in mid-2010 were beginning to regain some of the pricing power they lost during the previous two years, according to an August 2010 study by American Express Business Travel. The company noted that airfares "increased substantially" in the first half of 2010, compared to the same period in 2009.[93] The ATA said airline passenger revenue rose 20% in July 2010 compared to the same month in 2009, for the seven straight month of revenue growth.[94]

Hotels

The U.S. lodging sector, after a period of expansion, is experiencing a downturn. According to consulting firm Colliers PKF Hospitality Research, U.S. hotels experienced a nearly 36% decline in profitability in 2009 compared to the previous year.[95] The U.S. hotel occupancy rate declined to 55.1% in 2009, from 60.3% in 2008.[96]

While a number of analysts forecast improved results for the lodging sector in 2010, they caution that recovery could take some time. According STR Global, a leading travel research firm, hotel occupancy rates surged in some areas of the United States in early 2010, but prices were not rising as fast. American Express Business Travel said it had negotiated a 9.8% average rate reduction on hotel rooms for its business clients in 2010 compared to 2009. Overall, business- traveler rates were slightly down year-over-year in 2010.[97]

The hotel sector also faces problems of debt and overcapacity that will be difficult to work through, analysts say. Hotel developers expanded during the past several years, spurred on by increasing business and the availability of credit. Some hotel chains have restructured their debt, but that may be only a temporary reprieve. According to one analyst:

> We believe the likelihood that future demand growth will be lower than the recent past will eventually force the US hotel industry to adjust its growth projections sharply downward. For now, however, we think low interest rates and lax accounting standards at banks have enabled developers to continue to pursuer faster-than-needed supply growth and allowed marginal operators to stay in business. This is likely to dilute the pace of any 2010 recovery.[98]

Taxpayers have increasingly supported the hotel industry. According to consulting firm HVS International, just three hotel developments of 700 rooms or more, outside of those built by gaming and resort industries, were constructed without some form of public support between 1994 to 2004.[99]

Tourism taxes

States and localities levy taxes on tourism, in particular taxes on hotel rooms and automobile rentals, to finance convention centers, stadiums and hotels, tourism promotion boards and other initiatives. In recent months as the recession has reduced revenues from a number of sources, forcing many states and locales to cut spending to balance their budgets, some have voted to impose new tourism taxes to finance government services or special programs in danger of elimination.[100] According to the National Conference of State Legislatures, Hawaii, Nevada, New Hampshire, Oklahoma and Massachusetts enacted measures, taking effect during their 2010 fiscal years, that raised hotel taxes. South Dakota also increased its tourism tax.

There are signs, however, that businesses and consumers are pushing back. For example, legislation introduced in U.S. Congress would limit the ability of states and localities to impose future "discriminatory" taxes on automobile rentals (H.R. 4175). In testimony to the U.S. House Committee on the Judiciary, Subcommittee on Commercial and Administrative Law in June 2010, officials of the car rental industry said that governments in 43 states and the District of Columbia had levied 118 different excise taxes on car rentals in various jurisdictions, an 800% increase in the number of such taxes since 1990.[101] The National League of Cities, National Association of Counties, U.S. Conference of Mayors, and Government Finance Officers Association opposed the bill, saying it would unfairly pre-empt state authority.[102]

States and localities are also engaged in a legal battle with online travel booking companies such as Expedia and Travelocity over taxes on lodging accommodations. More than 40 cities have sued online travel companies, saying that the governments are entitled to collect hotel taxes on the full retail price that consumers pay the online booking companies for the rooms, not the lesser, discounted price negotiated between hotels and the online booking companies.[103] The online travel booking companies say the difference in pricing represents a service fee to the hotels for filling what could otherwise be empty rooms and has called on Congress to set national standards in the area.[104]

Tourism taxes in some areas have been used to help build conference and convention centers, which are considered by many cities as a key to economic development and growth. One prominent critic contends that cities around the country have entered into an expensive and unproductive "arms race," building expensive facilities to compete for declining trade shows, conventions and other business gatherings.[105] The industry has offered a sharp rebuttal of those criticisms.[106]

GULF COAST TOURISM

Though the overall U.S. travel and tourism sector has shown signs of improvement in 2010, after the steep decline in 2009, there is concern about the Gulf Coast. There have been reports that many would-be visitors have canceled vacation plans along coastal areas of Louisiana, Alabama, Mississippi, and Florida in response to the BP Deepwater Horizon oil spill, which began in April.[107]

Many businesses in the Gulf Coast states are heavily dependent on travel and tourism, particularly areas near the shore. The Federal Reserve Bank of Atlanta, which oversees the banking industry and monitors economic activity in much of the Southeast, estimates that 105,000 jobs are tied to travel and tourism in areas of the Gulf affected by the spill.[108] A study by the University of Western Florida estimated that more than 45,000 jobs were linked to tourism in the five Florida Gulf counties, with more than 10,000 tourism employees working in restaurants, 3,500 in hotel/motels and 1,200 in air travel. [109] The report noted that the oil spill hit the Gulf at a time when tourism revenues are at a seasonal peak—Memorial Day through August. (In downstate Florida where more tourists drive rather than fly to their destinations, the peak market period is January through April.)

State officials throughout the region have mounted aggressive public relations campaigns to offset negative publicity about the Gulf and have conducted their own consumer research. A study for the Louisiana Department of Culture, Recreation, and Tourism by Market Dynamics Research Group found 17% of what were identified as target visitors had canceled or delayed a trip to Louisiana because of the oil spill.[110] The study was based on the responses of 903 people in Mississippi, Texas and Florida, identified as target visitors based on age, income and other factors.

However, preliminary, hard data on the impact of the oil spill indicate that the economic fallout, while significant, may not be as severe as some had feared. The state of Florida in August reported that it hosted 20.8 million visitors in the second quarter of 2010, a 2.4% increase in domestic visitors and a 11.9% rise in international visitors from the same period in 2009, despite the fact that the BP oil spill affected bookings in some areas of the state. The state carried out an aggressive marketing campaign to mitigate traveler concerns about the state, financed in part by funding through BP.[111]

The Alabama Gulf Coast Convention and Visitors Bureau on August 3, 2010 released visitor figures for the Gulf Shores and Orange Beach area. The data show that taxable lodging rentals for May 2010 fell by 7.3% from the same month in 2009, while retail sales dipped 4.3% during the period.[112] Alabama is processing June data, and early indications are that overall hotel and condominium occupancy rates for the month could be down 20% to 30% from a year earlier. Condominium rentals appeared to have fallen more sharply than hotel occupancy.[113]

Hotel room, vacation rental and other vacation bookings may have increased elsewhere in the Southeastern United States, as vacationers searched for alternatives to Gulf Coast locations. In the end, while some regions of the Gulf Coast could be hurt, national tourism spending may not be much affected if tourists simply shift spending from vacation point A to point B.

The Federal Reserve Bank of Atlanta also notes that while new unemployment benefits claims in coastal areas increased somewhat in the weeks after the spill, unemployment claims at the end of June did not show large swings, possibly because BP hired out-of-work fishermen and others for cleanup efforts.[114]

LEGISLATIVE INITIATIVES

Though the travel and tourism sector is an important part of the national economy and many state economies, it does not usually rise to the top of the agenda in Congress in the way that other specific businesses or industries such as manufacturing or agriculture do. There are a number of reasons for the difference. Travel and tourism are not one industry but a measure of consumer purchases of products and services from across a broad spectrum of industries. The sector is made up of businesses—hotels, gaming, transportation companies, retailers and others—that may have competing interests in some areas. Regulation is dispersed. While there is an Office of Travel & Tourism Industries (OTTI) in the U.S. Department of Commerce, charged with improving the international competitiveness of the sector, travel and tourism fall under the purview of a number of federal agencies, including the U.S. Department of Transportation, the U.S. Department of State and the U.S. Department of Labor.

Still, as the U.S. Department of Commerce, industry groups and states have developed more comprehensive data on the economic impact of travel and tourism, legislators have introduced and enacted specific legislation to aid and regulate the sector. In March 2010, partly in response to steep downturn in travel in 2008 and 2009, President Obama signed into law, the Travel Promotion Act (P.L. 111-145). The law will create a public-private 11-member board, Corporation for Travel Promotion, to market the United States as a travel destination to overseas visitors. The board will have an estimated $100 million annual budget, funded by a $14 assessment on international visitors from the more than 30 nations that have U.S. visa waiver programs, meaning visitors from those nations do not have to obtain a visa for temporary travel to the United States. The travel and tourism industry under the law is also required to put up matching funds and services for the program.[115]

A group of lawmakers from Gulf Coast states have proposed measures to mitigate the impact of the oil spill on regional businesses through such strategies as tax credits to Gulf Coast firms that hire workers displaced by the oil spill and a program to reimburse Gulf states for lost revenue if they implement a hotel or car rental tax holiday to spur tourism.[116]

Other travel and tourism-related legislation in the 111th Congress includes H.R. 4676, the Travel Regional Investment Partnership Act, which would authorize $50 million in matching grants over five years to tourism marketing organizations. In July, President Obama signed The Cruise Vessel Safety and Security Act (P.L. 111-207) to institute new safety and other consumer protections on cruise ships.

But most congressional action that affects the travel and tourism sector—sometimes in a major way—is much more indirect. For example, the government affairs agenda of the U.S. Travel Association, an industry trade group, includes issues ranging from air traffic control modernization to global warming, public lands, pandemic and emergency response, highway construction, airport security and international trade issues.[117] Another major issue is border security, including visa requirements for visitors hoping to travel to the United States. Highway and other transportation programs, funding for national parks, and heritage sites, environmental and housing policies also play a role in the development of the industry.

Looking forward, the travel and tourism industry is becoming more technology-driven, with many bookings and sales now made on the Internet. That trend has fostered a dispute about taxation of tourism-related activities, in line with a broader debate about taxation of commerce on the Internet. States and localities have filed lawsuits against online travel booking companies regarding the level of taxes to be paid to governments for booking hotel accommodations online. The online booking industry has responded by suggesting that Congress intervene with legislation setting a federal standard.[118] In addition, the House Committee on the Judiciary, Subcommittee on Administrative and Commercial Law on June 15, 2010, held a hearing on H.R. 4175, which would limit the ability of states and localities to impose taxes on automobile rentals.[119] The fact that the debate over taxation of hotel rooms and of auto rental has made it to the halls of Congress suggests growing business and consumer frustration with states' strategy of taxing tourists to pay for state services.

APPENDIX A. TOURISM OUTPUT BY CATEGORY

Table A-1. Tourism Output by Category, 2007
(Millions of Dollars)

Commodity	Tourism-Related Output
Traveler accommodations	$206,876
Food services and drinking places	$232,497
Domestic passenger air transportation services	$110,344
International passenger air transportation services	$75,814
Passenger rail transportation services	$2,359
Passenger water transportation services	$18,315
Interurban bus transportation	$3,034
Interurban charter bus transportation	$1,398
Urban transit systems and other transportation services	$7,215
Taxi service.	$8,051
Scenic and sightseeing transportation services	$3,938
Automotive rental	$41,688
Other vehicle rental	$1,234
Automotive repair services	$19,935
Parking lots and garages	$3,378
Highway tolls	$1,380
Travel arrangement and reservation services	$63,875
Motion pictures and performing arts	$22,750
Spectator sports	$9,889
Participant sports	$20,154
Gambling	$58,183
All other recreation and entertainment	$29,196
Gasoline	$133,122
Nondurable PCE commodities other than gasoline	$232,616
Total	$1,307,237

Source: U.S. Department of Commerce, Bureau of Economic Analysis, *Travel and Tourism Satellite Accounts 2005-2008*, Table 5.

APPENDIX B. TOP 20 MARKETS FOR FOREIGN VISITORS TO THE UNITED STATES

Table B-1. Top 20 Markets for Foreign Visitors to United States

Data are for Calendar Year 2009
Canada
Mexico
United Kingdom
Japan
Germany
Brazil
France
Italy
Korea, South
Australia
Venezuela
Colombia
Spain
China & Hong Kong
Netherlands
Ireland
Sweden
India
Switzerland
Argentina

Source: U.S. Department of Commerce, *2009 Monthly Tourism Statistics.*

APPENDIX C. U.S. TRAVEL AND TOURISM EMPLOYMENT

Table C-1. U.S. Employment in Travel and Tourism Industry, 2007

Industry	Direct Employment (In Thousands)	Total Tourism-Related Employment (In Thousands)
Traveler accommodations	1,366	1,681
Nonfarm residential tenant occupied permanent site	11	33
Food services and drinking places	1,943	2,598
Air transportation services	452	801
Rail transportation services	10	19
Water transportation services	40	146
Interurban bus transportation	22	32
Interurban charter bus transportation	20	29
Urban transit systems and other transportation	69	99
Taxi service	55	79
Scenic and sightseeing transportation services	19	27
Automotive equipment rental and leasing	95	223
Automotive repair services	45	69
Parking lots and garages	15	31
Toll highways	5	9
Travel arrangement and reservation services	198	304
Motion pictures and performing arts	30	64
Spectator sports	65	110
Participant sports	241	311
Gambling	189	273
All other recreation and entertainment	126	195
Industries producing nondurable PCE (Personal Consumption Expenditure) commodities, excluding petroleum refineries	8	25
Petroleum refineries	153	441

Table C-1. (Continued)

Industry	Direct Employment (In Thousands)	Total Tourism-Related Employment (In Thousands)
Wholesale trade and transportation services	180	283
Gasoline service stations	78	94
Retail trade services, excluding gasoline service stations	395	474
All other industries	84	163
Total	**5,912**	**8,612**

Source: U.S. Department of Commerce, Bureau of Economic Analysis, *Travel and Tourism Satellite Accounts, 2005-2008*, Table 7.

Note: Data are the most recent detailed breakdowns available. Overall employment includes direct and indirect employment. Indirect employment counts jobs, for example, of people producing products such as sunscreen, scooters, and the like that are ultimately used by tourists.

End Notes

[1] Frederico Neto, *A New Approach to Sustainable Tourism Development: Moving Beyond Environmental Protection*, United Nations, DESA Discussion Paper, No. 29, March 2003, http://www.un.org/esa/desa/papers/2003/esa03dp29.pdf.

[2] United Nations World Tourism Organization, "Facts & Figures, Historical Perspective of World Tourism," Information Sheet, http://www.unwto.org/facts/eng/historical/htm.

[3] United Nations World Tourism Organization, "Facts & Figures, Historical Perspective of World Tourism," Information Sheet; UNWTO, "Tourism 2020 Vision," Fact Sheet, http://www.world-tourism

[4] U.S. Department of Commerce, Bureau of Economic Analysis, "Travel and Tourism Spending Turns Up in First Quarter 2010," Press Release, June 22, 2010, *http://www.bea.gov/ newsreleases/industry/tourism*

[5] U.S. Department of Commerce, International Trade Administration, "Key Facts about International Travel and Tourism To the United States," Fact Sheet, 2009.

[6] Eric S. Griffith and Steven L. Zemanek, U.S. Department of Commerce, Bureau of Economic Affairs, "U.S. Travel and Tourism Satellite Accounts for 2005-2008," *Survey of Current Business*, June 2009, Table J, http://www.bea.gov/ scb/pdf/2009/06%20June/0609_travel-text.pdf.

[7] U.S. Department of Commerce, International Trade Administration, "Key Facts about International Travel and Tourism To the United States," Fact Sheet, 2009, http://tinet.ita.doc.gov/outreachpages/download_data_table/ 2009_Key_Facts.pdf.

[8] U.S. Department of Commerce, International Trade Administration, *U.S. Travel and Tourism Industries, A Year in Review, (2009)*, http://tinet.ita.doc.gov/pdf/2009-year-in-review.pdf.

[9] Ibid.

[10] Interactive Travel Services Association, http://www.interactivetravel.org/IndustryBackground/IB_MoreInformation.asp?IB=Hotel%20Occupancy%20Taxes&IndustryBackground=10008.

[11] Columb Higgins, "Senator Menendez: Offshore drilling is a threat to Jersey Shore," June 9, 2010, *Shore News Today*, http://www.shorenewstoday.com/index.php/ocean-city-mainmenu/ocean-city-general-news/1474-senatormenendez-offshore-drilling-is-a-threat-to-jersey-shore.html.

[12] Roger Yu, "Companies criticize U.S. travel visa process," *USA Today*, September 3, 2010, http://travel.usatoday.com/news/2010-08-31-businesstravel31_ST_N.htm.

[13] Richard Butler, Department of Hospitality and Tourism Management, Strathclyde Business School, University of Strathclyde, Glasgow, "Tourism in the Future: Cycles, Waves or Wheels," *Futures*, August 2009.

[14] Dennis R. Judd and Susan S. Fainstein, Editors, *The Tourist City*, Pub. 1999, Running Fret Books, Morrisville NC, (Yale University with assistance from the Louis Stern Memorial Fund), p. 1.

[15] Brandon Dupont, Alka Gandhi and Thomas J. Weiss, *The American Invasion of Europe: The Long Term Rise in Overseas Travel: 1820-2000*, NBER Working Paper No. 13977, National Bureau of Economic Research, April 2008, p. 8, *http://www.nber.org/papers/w13977.pdf.*

[16] Ibid.

[17] Richard Butler, Department of Hospitality and Tourism Management, Strathclyde Business School, University of Strathclyde, Glasgow, "Tourism in the Future: Cycles, Waves or Wheels," *Futures*, August 2009.

[18] Eric S. Griffith and Steven L. Zemanek, U.S. Department of Commerce, Bureau of Economic Affairs, "U.S. Travel and Tourism Satellite Accounts for 2005-2008," *Survey of Current Business*, June 2009.

[19] Heywood T. Sanders, *Space Available: The Realities of Convention Centers as Economic Development Strategy*, Brookings Institution, January 2005, http://www.brookings.edu/reports/2005/01cities_sanders.aspx.

[20] Sumiye Okubo and Mark A. Planting, "U.S. Travel and Tourism Satellite Accounts for 1992," *Survey of Current Business*, U.S. Department of Commerce, Bureau of Economic Analysis, July 1998, *http://www.bea.gov/scb/* account _articles/national/0798ied/maintext.htm.

[21] Ibid. The TSA system has also been endorsed by the Organization for Economic Cooperation and Development, the World Trade Organization and EUROSTAT, the European statistical organization, among others.

[22] Victor T.C. Middleton, Alan Fyall, Michael Morgan, Ashok Ranchhod, *Marketing in Travel and Tourism,* Butterworth-Heinemann Publishers, Mass., Fourth Edition, 2009, p. 9. The UNWTO defines visitors as persons traveling to and staying in places outside their usual environment for not more than one consecutive year for leisure, business and other purposes not related to the exercise of an activity remunerated from within the place visited. The U.S. Commerce Department precise definition of visitor is someone who travels out of his or her usual environment, which is the area of normal, everyday activities within 50-100 miles of home, for a period less than one year or who stays overnight in a hotel or motel.

[23] This report will use the term visitors when describing BEA data, but will use visitors, tourists, and travelers interchangeably elsewhere for ease of reading.

[24] Brandon Dupont, Alka Gandhi and Thomas J. Weiss, *The American Invasion of Europe: The Long Term Rise in Overseas Travel: 1820-2000*, NBER Working Paper No. 13977, National Bureau of Economic Research, April 2008, p. 7.

[25] Ibid. The UNWTO has data breaking down travel into trips for leisure, recreation and holidays, business and professional purposes and other purposes such as visiting friends and relatives, health treatment or religious reasons. Likewise, businesses and nonprofit groups have other measures of travel.

[26] Sumiye Okubo and Mark A. Planting, "U.S. Travel and Tourism Satellite Accounts for 1992," *Survey of Current Business*, U.S. Department of Commerce, Bureau of Economic Analysis, July 1998, http://www.bea.gov/scb/ account _articles/national/0798ied/maintext.htm.

[27] Eric S. Griffith and Steven L. Zemanek, U.S. Department of Commerce, Bureau of Economic Affairs, "U.S. Travel and Tourism Satellite Accounts for 2005-2008," *Survey of Current Business*, June 2009, Table 5.

[28] U.S. Department of Commerce, Bureau of Economic Analysis, "Travel and Tourism Spending Turns Up in First Quarter 2010," Press Release, June 22, 2010, Table 3. The BEA estimates that the travel and tourism sector generates 3% of U.S. Gross Domestic Product, the broadest measure of goods and services produced in the nation. The BEA figure is based on a value-added measure of GDP, rather than only accounting for final demand.

[29] Sumiye Okubo, Barbara M. Fraumeni, and Mahnaz Fahim-Nader, "A Proposal To Include Motor Vehicle Services in the U.S. Travel and Tourism Satellite Accounts," *Survey of Current Business*, June 2007, http://bea.gov/scb/pdf/2007/ 06%20June/0607_vehicles.pdf.

[30] UNWTO, *Measuring the Economic Importance of the Meetings Industry, Developing a Tourism Satellite Account Extension*, 2006, *http://www.mpiweb.org/CMS/uploadedFiles/ Foundation/Foundation_Europe/*Measuring%20the%20econonmic%20Importance%20of% 20Meetings%20Inudustry.pdf.

[31] U.S. Department of Commerce, International Trade Administration, "Key Facts about International Travel and Tourism To the United States," Fact Sheet.

[32] Ibid.

[33] World Travel & Tourism Council, *Travel & Tourism Economic Impact, 2010, Executive Summary*, http://www.wttc.org/bin/pdf/original_pdf_file/2010_exec_summary_final.pdf.

[34] U.S. Department of Commerce, International Trade Administration, *U.S. Travel and Tourism Industries: A Year in Review, 2009*. Commerce has been keeping records on trade-related spending since 1960.

[35] U.S. Travel Association, "Travel Industry Hails Senate Effort to Improve Visa Processing For Foreign Visitors," Press Release, July 29, 2010, http://www.ustravel.org/news/press-releases/travel-industry-hails-senate-effort-improvevisa-processing-foreign-visitors.

[36] CRS Report R41 104, *Immigration Visa Issuances and Grounds for Exclusion: Policy and Trends*, by Ruth Ellen Wasem. For additional information, see CRS Report RL32221, *Visa Waiver Program*, by Alison Siskin.

[37] U.S. Department of Labor, Bureau of Labor Statistics, *Spotlight on Travel*, http://www.bls.gov/spotlight/2010/travel/ pdf/travel.pdf.

[38] U.S. Department of Commerce, Bureau of Economic Affairs, "Travel and Tourism Spending Turns Up in First Quarter 2010," Press Release, June 22, 2010.

[39] Ibid.

[40] According to the U.S. Labor Department, Bureau of Labor Statistics, there were an average of about 140 million employed individuals in the United States in first quarter of 2010.

[41] World Travel & Tourism Council, *Travel and Tourism Economic Impact 2010*, Executive Summary, p. 3. Some industry groups and analysts have their own estimates of travel and tourism employment that are larger than the figures produced by the BEA. For example, the U.S. Travel Association, a trade group representing a wide range of businesses in travel and tourism estimates that 10.1 million U.S. workers are directly or indirectly employed in the sector. The group also produces its own state employment figures, estimating that one in every nine nonfarm jobs in the United States is directly or indirectly induced by travel or tourism. This report uses BEA and U.S. Department of Labor figures, however, not just for travel and tourism but for other economic measures.

[42] U.S. Department of Labor, Bureau of Labor Statistics, *Spotlight on Travel: Chart Data*.

[43] U.S. Department of Labor, Bureau of Labor Statistics, Occupational Employment Statistics, http://www.bls.gov/oes/ current/oes372012.htm.

[44] World Sport Destination Expo and *Sport Travel News*, "Sport Tourism," Fact Sheet.

[45] Daniel Boyette, "Beach sports revenue numbers booming," *Mobile Press-Register*, August 1, 2010, http://blog.al.com/live/2010/08/post_75.html.

[46] National Trust for Historic Preservation, "Cultural Heritage Tourism 2010 Fact Sheet," http://www.preservationnation.org/issues/heritage-tourism

[47] CRS Report RL3 3462, *Heritage Areas: Background, Proposals, and Current Issues*, by Carol Hardy Vincent.

[48] U.S. Department of Interior, Bureau of Land Management, http://www.blm.gov/wo/st/en/res/Education_in_BLM/Learning_Landscapes/For_Teachers/Heritage_Education.html.

[49] The International Ecotourism Society, "Certificate in Sustainable Tourism Management," http://www.ecotourism.org/site/c.orLQKXPCLmF/b.4835383/k.30FE/Certificate_in_Sustainable_Tourism_Management__The_International_Ecotourism_Society.htm.

[50] George Washington University School of Business, Tourism and Hospitality Management, "Ecotourism Management," http://business.gwu.edu/tourism

[51] Hans Detlefsen and Nina Vetter, *Convention Centers: Is the Industry Overbuilt?*, HVS Reports, February 25, 2008, http://www.hospitalitynet.org/file/152003300.pdf.

[52] Medical Tourism Association, http://www.medicaltourismassociation.com/en/index.html.

[53] Health Options Worldwide, "Medical Tourism Agency Health Options Worldwide Discusses the Benefits of Domestic Medical Travel Within the United States," Press Release, PR Newswire, August 10, 2010, http://www.prnewswire.com/news-releases/medical-tourism-

[54] Jeffrey C. Bauer, "Medical tourism wave of the future in a world of hurt?" *Health Care Financial Management*, August 2009.

[55] Virginia Cooperative Extension, Virginia Tech and Virginia State University, *Agri-Tourism*, http://pubs.ext.vt.edu/ 310/310-003/3 10-003.html.

[56] Penny Leff, "First statewide agritourism survey yields early results," *Small Farm News*, Cooperative Extension Service, University of California, Vol. 2., 2009.

[57] Brandon Dupont, Alka Gandhi and Thomas J. Weiss, *The American Invasion of Europe: The Long Term Rise in Overseas Travel: 1820-2000*, NBER Working Paper No. 13977, National Bureau of Economic Research, April 2008, p. 37.

[58] United Nations World Tourism Organization, "DECLARATION: Harnessing Tourism for the Millennium Development Goals," September 13, 2005, http://www.world-tourism

[59] Dain Bolwell and Wolfgang Weinz, *Reducing Poverty Through Tourism*, International Labour Organization, October 2008, p. 6, *http://www.ilo.org/public/english/dialogue/sector/papers/tourism*

[60] Office of New York Mayor Michael Bloomberg, "Mayor Bloomberg Announces New York City Was 2009's Most Popular U.S. Tourist Destination For First Time in Nearly 20 Years As Leisure and Hospitality Jobs Surpass Pre- Recession Levels," Press Release, January 4, 2010.

[61] VisitFlorida.com, "Estimated 22.7 Million Visited Florida in First Quarter of 2010," Press Release, May 20, 2010, http://media

[62] State of Hawaii, Department of Business, Economic Development and Tourism, *Research and Data Highlights, Third Quarter, 2010*, http://hawaii.gov/dbedt/info/economic/highlights/read-highlights-2010-3q.pdf.

[63] The Center for Business and Economic Research, University of Nevada, Las Vegas, "Metropolitan Las Vegas Tourism Statistics," Fact Sheet.

[64] U.S. Department of Commerce, International Trade Administration, *Overseas Visitation Estimates for U.S. States, Cities, and Census Regions: 2009*, http://tinet.ita.doc.gov/outreachpages/download_data_table/2009 _States _and _Cities.pdf. The data do not include visitors from Canada and Mexico. Canada is the top market for visitors to the United States.

[65] Chad Wilkerson, Kansas City Federal Reserve Bank, "Travel and Tourism: An Overlooked Industry in the U.S. and Tenth District," *Economic Review*, http://www.kansascityfed.org/publicat/econrev/PDF/3q03wilk.pdf.

[66] Richard Deitz, Federal Reserve Bank of New York, "Tourism's Role in the Upstate New York Economy," *The Regional Economy*, Spring 2004, *http://www.newyorkfed.org/research/ regional_economy*

[67] IHS Global Insight and D.K. Shifflet & Associates, *Public Tourism PromotionROI: Cutting the Promotional Budget is Tempting, Is it Worth It?*, February 2009, p. 4, http://www.state.sd.us/bfm/econ/TourismROI0209.pdf.

[68] Phil Davies, Federal Reserve Bank of Minneapolis, "A nice place to visit, but ...," *fedgazette*, May 2009, http://www.minneapolisfed.org/publications_papers/pub_display.cfm?id=4172.

[69] Dave Marcouiller, University of Wisconsin, Madison/Extension, "'Boosting' Tourism as Rural Public Policy: Panacea or Pandora's Box," *The Journal of Regional Analysis Policy*, Special Issue on State Rural Development Policy, 2007.

[70] CRS Report RL32647, *Government Advertisement of Tourism: Recent Action and Longstanding Controversies*, by Kevin R. Kosar.

[71] U.S. International Trade Administration, "Travel Promotion Act 2009," Fact Sheet, http://trade.gov/press/pressreleases/2010/travel-promotion-act-2009-factsheet. asp.

[72] Chad Wilkerson, Federal Reserve Bank of Kansas City, "Travel and Tourism: An Overlooked Industry in the U.S. and Tenth District," *Economic Review,* May 2003, p. 50.

[73] Ibid, p. 51.

[74] U.S. Department of Commerce, International Trade Administration, *U.S. Travel and Tourism Industries, A Year in Review (2009)*, http://tinet.ita.doc.gov/pdf/2009-year-in-review.pdf.

[75] UNWTO, "Tourism and the World Economy," http://www.unwto.org/facts/eng/economy

[76] Dawn Gilbertson, "Arizona's immigration law has little impact on Arizona's tourism," *The Arizona Republic*, July 28, 2010.

[77] Mark Lewis, "The AIG Effect," *Forbes*, February 16, 2010, http://www.forbes.com/ 2010/02/16/aig-business-travelleadership-meetings-1 0-corporate-conferences.html.

[78] Dave Arnold, "Meetings Stigma Impacts Conference Centers," Colliers PFK Consulting USA, Report Summary, http://www.pkfc.com/en/pkfhome/FreeStuff/Newsletter/HMU_201007-1.aspx.

[79] Ibid.

[80] Richard Deitz, Federal Reserve Bank of New York, "Tourism's Role in the Upstate New York Economy," *The Regional Economy*, Spring 2004.

[81] John H. Tibbetts, "The Coast's Great Leap," *Coastal Heritage*, Vol. 19, No. 2, Fall 2004.

[82] Russell Pearlman, "Municipal Bonds: Derailed," *SmartMoney* Magazine, May 17, 2010, http://www.smartmoney.com/investing/bondsutm_campaign=Feed%3A+smartmoney%2Fh eadlines+(SmartMoney.com)&print=1; Wells Fargo, "Notice of Bankruptcy Filing to Holders of Director of the State of Nevada Department of Business and Industry Las Vegas Monorail Project Revenue Bonds," January 14, 2010, http://www.bondview.com/blog/wp-content/uploads/las-vegasmonorail-default.pdf.

[83] Samuel Mendlinger and Tomoko Tsundoda, "Economic and Social Impact of Tourism on a Small Town: Peterborough New Hampshire," *Journal of Service Science and Management*, June 2009.

[84] CRS Report RL32450, *Cruise Ship Pollution: Background, Laws and Regulations, and Key Issues*, by Claudia Copeland.

[85] Richard J. Reeder and Dennis M. Brown, *Recreation, Tourism and Rural Well-Being*, U.S. Department of Agriculture, Economic Research Service, Economic Research Report #7, August 2005, p. 1, http://www.ers.usda.gov/ Publications/err7/. The study noted that the recreation and non-recreation counties had similar populations. The recreation counties on average had lower population density.

[86] Ibid.

[87] Ibid, p. 24.

[88] *Lake Tahoe Basin Prosperity Plan Executive Summary*, http://www.tahoechamber.org/Admin/ Uploads/Executive_Summary_Meeting_2010-08-13.pdf.

[89] Matthew Renda, "The 21st century Tahoe tourist wants to play in the woods and at the blackjack tables, economists say," *Tahoe Daily Tribune*, July 30, 2010, http://www.tahoedailytribune.com/article/20100730/NEWS/100739999/1005&parentprofile =1056.

[90] Eric S. Griffith and Steven L Zemanek, U.S. Department of Commerce, Bureau of Economic Affairs, "U.S. Travel and Tourism Satellite Accounts for 2005-2008," *Survey of Current Business*, June 2009, Table 7.

[91] U.S. Department of Transportation, "June Passenger Airline Employment Data: June 2010 Employment Down 2.4 Percent from June 2009," Press Release, August 17, 2010, http://www.bts.gov/press_releases/2010/bts040_10/pdf/ bts040_10.pdf.

[92] Air Transport Association, *2010 Economic Report: When America Flies, It Works*, p. 9, http://www.airlines.org/ Economics/ReviewOutlook/Documents/2010AnnualReport.pdf.

[93] American Express Business Travel, "Airline Suppliers Regaining Pricing Power over Business Travelers in the First Half of 2010, Reports American Express Business Travel Monitor," Press Release, August 10, 2010, http://www.hospitalitynet.org/news/ 4047836.search?queryairline+suppliers+regaining+pricing+power+over+business+travelers +in+the+first+half+of+2010%2c+reports+americ an+express+business+travel+monitor.

[94] Air Transport Association, "U.S. Airlines Post Seventh Consecutive Month of Revenue Growth in Recovering Economy," Press Release, August 19, 2010.

[95] Robert Mandelbaum, PFK Hospitality Research, "Nine of Ten Hotels Lost Profits in 2009," PFK Consulting USA, *http://www.pkfc.com/en/pkfhome/FreeStuff/IndustryReports/ IR2010_06A.aspx*.

[96] Mark Basham and Esther Y. Kwon, *Industry Surveys, Lodging & Gaming*, Standard & Poor's, May 20, 2010, p. 5.

[97] American Express Business Travel, "Airline Suppliers Regaining Pricing Power over Business Travelers in the First Half of 2010, Reports American Express Business Travel Monitor," Press Release, August 10, 2010.

[98] Mark Basham and Esther Y. Kwon, *Industry Surveys, Lodging & Gaming*, Standard & Poor's, May 20, 2010, p. 5.

[99] Thomas Hazinski, Managing Director, HVS Convention, Sport, & Entertainment Facilities Consulting, *Public Involvement In Hotel Financing*, October 28, 2004.

[100] National Conference on State Legislatures, "Actions & Proposals to Balance the FY 2010 Budget: Other Revenue Actions, Taxes/Fees," *http://www.ncsl.org/default.aspx?tabid= 17252*.

[101] Testimony of Raymond T. Wagner, Jr., On Behalf of Enterprise Holdings, Inc. and The Coalition Against Discriminatory Car Rental Excise Taxes, US. House Committee on the Judiciary, Subcommittee on Commercial and Administrative Law, June 15, 2010, http://judiciary

[102] Testimony of Timothy Firestine, Chief Administrative Officer, Montgomery County, Maryland On Behalf Of National League of Cities, National Association of Counties, U.S. Conference of Mayors, and Government Finance Officers Association, US. House Committee on the Judiciary, Subcommittee on Commercial and Administrative Law, June 15, 2010, http://judiciary

[103] Alan Greenblatt, "Cities, Websites And Hotels At Odds Over Taxes," *NPR*, August 25, 2010, http://www.npr.org/ templates/story/story.php?storyId= 128 847984.

[104] Brad Tuttle, "Taxing controversy: Should hotels or booking engines be paying more in taxes?," *Budget Travel*, July 8, 2010, http://current.newsweek.com/budgettravel/2010/07/ taxing_controversy_should_hote.html.

[105] Heywood T. Sanders, *Space Available: The Realities of Convention Centers as Economic Development Strategy*, Brookings Institution, January 2005, *http://www.brookings.edu/ reports/2005/01cities_sanders.aspx*.

[106] Thomas Hazinski and Hans Detlefsen, HVS Convention, Sports, & Entertainment Facilities Consulting, "Is the Sky Falling on the Convention Center Industry," HVS Journal May 2005, http://www.hotel-online.com/News/PR2005_2nd/ May05 _ConventionBiz.html.

[107] CRS Report R41262, *Deep water Horizon Oil Spill: Selected Issues for Congress*, coordinated by Curry L. Hagerty and Jonathan L. Ramseur.

[108] Federal Reserve Bank of Atlanta, "Is the Worst Over for Gulf Tourism," *Southpoint*, August 4, 2010. http://southpoint.frbatlanta.org/.

[109] Rick Harper, Director of The Haas Center for Business Research and Economic Development *The Economic Impact to Northwest Florida of the Deep water Horizon Oil Spill*, University of West Florida, June 2010, p. 4.

[110] Louisiana Office of Tourism (Market Dynamics), *Regional Effects on Perception/BP Oil Spill Survey Wave 1 Results*, June 30, 2010, *http://www.crt.louisiana.gov/tourism*Regional EffectsonPerception_BPOilSpillSurveyWave1Results 20100630.pdf.

[111] VisitFlorida.com, "Estimated 20.8 Million Visited Florida in Second Quarter 2010," Press Release, August 23, 2010, http://media

[112] Alabama Gulf Coast Convention and Visitors Bureau, "Alabama Beaches Release Tourism Figures for First Half of Summer," Press Release, August 3, 2010, http://www.gulfshores.com/pressroom/release.aspx?ID=484.

[113] Ibid.

[114] Federal Reserve Bank of Atlanta, Regional Economic Information Network, *http://www.frbatlanta.org/rein.*

[115] U.S. Customs and Border Protection, "DHS, CBP Announce Interim Final Rule for ESTA Fee," Press Release, August 6, 2010. Of the fee, $4 will be for administrative purposes and $10 to fund the tourism program.

[116] Sen. Mary Landrieu, "Landrieu Proposes Tax Breaks and Tourism Boost for Gulf Coast Residents, Business," Press Release, July 2, 2010.

[117] U.S. Travel Association, http://www.ustravel.org/government-affairs/domestic-policy-issues.

[118] Jeri Clausing, "Online giants take their hotel-tax battle to consumers," *Travel Weekly*, July 12, 2010.

[119] House Committee on the Judiciary, Subcommittee on Administrative and Commercial Law, Hearing on: H.R. 4175, the End Discriminatory State Taxes for Automobile Renters Act of 2009, http://judiciary hear_100615_1.html.

In: United States Travel and Tourism Industry   ISBN: 978-1-61209-111-2
Editors: D.P. Moore and A.G. Doherty   © 2011 Nova Science Publishers, Inc.

Chapter 2

TRAVEL AND TOURISM SPENDING GROWS IN SECOND QUARTER 2010[*]

Bureau of Economic Analysis
U.S. Department of Commerce

Real spending on travel and tourism increased at an annual rate of 3.0 percent in 2010:2, following an increase of 5.0 percent (revised) in 2010:1. By comparison, real gross domestic product (GDP) increased 1.6 percent (second estimate) in 2010:2 after increasing 3.7 percent in 2010:1. Travel and tourism prices increased 2.7 percent in 2010:2 after increasing 4.1 percent (revised) in 2010:1.

- Passenger air transportation spending increased 3.9 percent in 2010:2 and 4.0 percent in 2010:1.
- Accommodations spending decelerated, increasing 6.1 percent in 2010:2 after increasing 13.4 percent in 2010:1.
- Prices for accommodations turned up in 2010:2, increasing 19.0 percent, after decreasing 6.4 percent in 2010:1.

---

[*] This is an edited, reformatted and augmented of a Bureau of Economic Analysis United States Department of Commerce, dated September 23, 2010.

After eight consecutive quarters of declines, direct tourism-related employment turned up, increasing 2.2 percent in 2010:2. By comparison, overall U.S. employment increased 2.2 percent in 2010:2 and increased 0.2 percent in 2010:1.

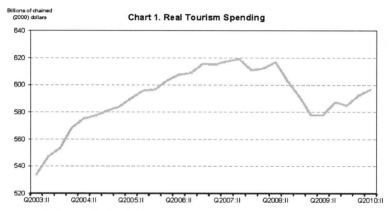

U.S. Bureau of Economic Analysis

Real Tourism Spending. Real spending on passenger air transportation increased 3.9 percent in 2010:2 as demand improved. Real spending on traveler accommodations slowed, increasing 6.1 percent after increasing more than 13 percent in 2010:1.

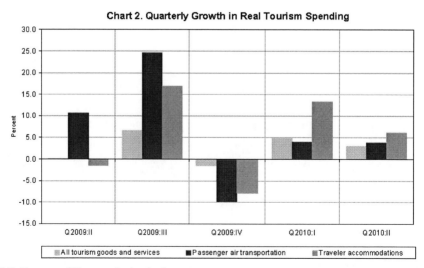

U.S. Bureau of Economic Analysis

Tourism Prices. Prices for passenger air transportation continued their strong growth, rising 16.0 percent in 2010:2. Prices for traveler accommodations showed a sharp upturn, increasing 19.0 percent in 2010:2 after decreasing 6.4 percent in 2010:1. Higher occupancy rates created pricing opportunities for hotels.

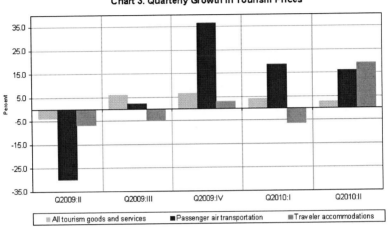

Chart 3. Quarterly Growth in Tourism Prices

U.S. Bureau of Economic Analysis

Tourism Employment. Overall growth in travel and tourism employment was 2.2 percent in 2010:2 — the first increase since 2008:1. In 2010:2, employment increased 0.5 percent in air transportation services and 4.7 percent in traveler accommodations.

Total Tourism-Related Spending. The U.S. production generated by tourism spending not only includes the goods and services that are purchased directly, but also the inputs used to produce these goods and services — indirect tourism-related spending. In 2010:2, total current-dollar tourism-related spending was $1.3 trillion and consisted of $750.9 billion (57 percent) of direct tourism spending — goods and services sold directly to visitors — and $575.3 billion (43 percent) of indirect tourism-related spending — goods and services used to produce what visitors buy.

Total Tourism-Related Employment. In 2010:2, total tourism-related employment was 8.1 million and consisted of 5.6 million (69 percent) direct tourism jobs — jobs where workers produce goods and services sold directly to visitors — and 2.5 million (31 percent) indirect tourism-related jobs — jobs where workers produce goods and services used to produce what visitors buy.

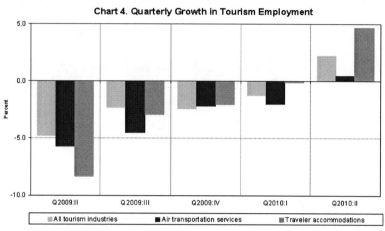

Chart 4. Quarterly Growth in Tourism Employment

U.S. Bureau of Economic Analysis

DEFINITIONS

Tourism spending. Tourism spending comprises all goods and services purchased by tourists (defined as people who travel for any reason). In the following tables, tourism spending is referred to as direct tourism output.

Indirect tourism-related spending. Indirect tourism-related spending comprises all output used as inputs in the process of producing direct tourism output (e.g., toiletries for hotel guests and the plastic used to produce souvenir key chains).

Total tourism-related spending. Total tourism-related spending is the sum of direct tourism spending and indirect tourism-related spending.

Direct tourism employment. Direct tourism employment comprises all jobs where the workers are engaged in the production of direct tourism output (such as hotel staff, airline pilots, and souvenir sellers).

Indirect tourism-related employment. Indirect tourism-related employment comprises all jobs where the workers are engaged in the production of indirect tourism-related output (e.g., employees of companies that produce toiletries for hotel guests and the plastic used to produce souvenir key chains).

Total tourism-related employment. Total tourism-related employment is the sum of direct tourism employment and indirect tourism-related employment.

These statistics are from BEA's Travel and Tourism Satellite Accounts (TTSAs), which are supported by funding from the Office of Travel and Tourism Industries, International Trade Administration, U.S. Department of Commerce. The current-price statistics of direct tourism output were derived from BEA's annual TTSAs (revised in June 2009) and from current-price quarterly statistics of personal consumption expenditures from the National Income and Product Accounts (NIPAs). The real statistics of direct tourism output were developed using price indexes from the Bureau of Labor Statistics (BLS) and real quarterly statistics of personal consumption expenditures from the NIPAs. The statistics of direct tourism employment were derived from the annual TTSAs (revised in June 2009) from BEA, the Quarterly Census of Employment and Wages (QCEW), and Current Employment Statistics (CES) from BLS.

Quarterly statistics are seasonally adjusted and expressed at annual rates, unless otherwise specified. Percent changes are calculated from unrounded data and annualized. Real values are in chained (2000) dollars. Price indexes are chain-type measures. Growth in overall U.S. employment is calculated using BLS total nonfarm employment from Current Employment Statistics, *www.bls.gov/ces/home.htm#data*.

These Travel and Tourism statistics do not reflect the results of the comprehensive revision of the annual industry accounts, released on May 25, 2010. They will be updated to incorporate this revision in Fall 2010.

Next release – Travel and Tourism statistics for third quarter 2010 will be released on Monday, December 20, 2010 at 8:30 a.m. EST.

BEA's national, international, regional, and industry statistics; the *Survey of Current Business*; and BEA news releases are available without charge on BEA's Web site at www.bea.gov. By visiting the site, you can also subscribe to receive free e-mail summaries of BEA releases and announcements

Table 1.a. Percent Change in Real Tourism Output [Percent change from preceding period]

Tourism - Goods and Services Group	2005	2006	2007	2008	2009	Seasonally adjusted at annual rates													
						Q-2007:I	Q-2007:II	Q-2007:III	Q-2007:IV	Q-2008:I	Q-2008:II	Q-2008:III	Q-2008:IV	Q-2009:I	Q-2009:II	Q-2009:III	Q-2009:IV	Q-2010:I	Q-2010:II
Traveler accommodations	3.1	4.1	3.1	1.6	-6.1	2.5	0.4	-1.3	10.1	-9.1	19.5	-3.1	-10.4	-21.8	-1.5	16.9	-7.9	13.4	6.1
Transportation	2.4	1.6	1.1	-3.3	-5.0	0.4	4.2	2.6	-15.4	9.3	-4.3	-13.2	-6.7	-14.4	3.9	13.7	-2.4	1.8	6.1
Passenger -air transportation	2.2	0.6	2.1	-6.8	-7.8	-0.5	13.3	2.5	-26.8	21.6	-17.9	-21.4	-8.7	-21.5	10.7	24.5	-9.8	4.0	3.9
All other transportation—related commodities	2.6	2.2	0.4	-1.1	-3.2	0.9	-1.2	2.6	-7.7	2.6	4.8	-8.2	-5.5	-9.7	0.2	8.1	2.0	0.6	7.5
Food services and drinking places	5.0	3.6	0.9	-0.5	-2.5	-0.8	1.9	0.4	0.5	-1.2	3.9	-6.0	-5.9	0.8	-2.8	-4.2	-0.3	7.0	2.2
Recreation, entertainment, and shopping	1.8	3.6	0.1	-1.8	-1.8	-2.7	-1.6	0.7	-2.3	-2.5	3.3	-6.7	-7.9	2.2	-1.5	-0.6	3.2	3.3	-2.4
Recreation and entertainment	0.7	2.0	0.6	-2.9	-1.0	-3.1	-2.3	2.8	-4.5	-6.1	1.4	-6.4	-2.8	3.2	-0.4	-3.7	0.5	1.5	-7.4
Shopping	2.9	4.7	-0.4	-1.0	-2.4	-2.4	-1.1	-0.8	-0.5	0.3	4.7	-6.9	-11.6	1.4	-2.3	1.8	5.2	4.7	1.4
All tourism goods and services	2.8	2.9	1.1	-1.6	-3.9	-0.3	1.5	1.0	-5.1	0.9	2.9	-8.6	-7.6	-8.9	0.2	6.6	-1.5	5.0	3.0

Source: U.S. Bureau of Economic Analysis

Table 1.b. Real Tourism Output [Millions of chained (2000) dollars]

Tourism Goods and Services Group	2005	2006	2007	2008	2009	Q2007:I	Q2007:II	Q2007:III	Q2007:IV	Q2008:I	Q2008:II	Q2008:III	Q2008:IV	Q2009:I	Q2009:II	Q2009:III	Q2009:IV	Q2010:I	Q2010:II
Traveler accommodations	100,356	104,473	107,721	109,420	102,713	107,168	107,262	106,925	109,531	106,948	111,827	110,959	107,944	101,517	101,140	105,169	103,025	106,324	107,916
Transportation	230,305	234,020	236,578	228,785	217,430	236,451	238,891	240,413	230,558	235,739	233,165	225,056	221,178	212,721	214,777	221,791	220,432	221,429	224,739
Passenger air transportation	101,613	102,255	104,413	97,298	89,733	103,627	106,918	107,585	99,523	104,510	99,474	93,662	91,547	86,170	88,391	93,376	90,994	91,890	92,773
All other transportation-related commodities	128,930	131,778	132,365	130,864	126,660	132,889	132,497	133,352	130,722	131,563	133,117	130,308	128,468	125,228	125,282	127,757	128,375	128,565	130,900
Food services and drinking places	96,015	99,492	100,399	99,921	97,399	99,969	100,433	100,536	100,659	100,348	101,321	99,767	98,249	98,456	97,768	96,727	96,647	98,287	98,820
Recreation entertainment, and shopping	160,598	166,305	166,395	163,377	160,385	166,982	166,316	166,618	165,664	164,621	165,967	163,131	159,791	160,646	160,033	159,800	161,060	162,386	161,404
Recreation and entertainment	68,678	70,043	70,491	68,427	67,744	70,751	70,346	70,840	70,027	68,928	69,171	68,042	67,568	68,094	68,022	67,390	67,469	67,721	66,424
Shop-ping	96,877	101,472	101,080	100,101	97,651	101,425	101,153	100,938	100,804	100,884	102,056	100,254	97,211	97,554	96,981	97,408	98,660	99,796	100,136
All tourism goods and services	591,711	608,899	615,772	605,980	582,080	615,250	617,597	619,178	611,066	612,446	616,899	603,172	591,405	577,814	578,041	587,317	585,147	592,311	596,753

Seasonally adjusted at annual rates

Source: U.S. Bureau of Economic Analysis.

Table 1.c. Percent Changes in Chain-Type Price Indexes for Direct Tourism Output
[Percent change from preceding period]

Tourism Goods and Services Group	2005	2006	2007	2008	2009	Seasonally adjusted at annual rates													
						Q-2007:I	Q-2007:II	Q-2007:III	Q-2007:IV	Q2008:I	Q2008:II	Q2008:III	Q2008:IV	Q2009:I	Q2009:II	Q2009:III	Q2009:IV	Q2010:I	Q2010:II
Traveler accommodations	5.7	3.7	4.8	0.2	-6.7	3.9	8.8	9.3	-2.8	0.9	-6.5	5.0	-7.0	-15.1	-6.8	-4.7	3.1	-6.4	19.0
Transportation	7.0	6.9	3.5	8.5	-9.6	5.6	11.7	5.8	15.6	8.3	14.3	18.8	-35.0	-22.1	-8.3	17.5	15.6	13.6	-1.6
Passenger air transportation	4.8	6.4	1.8	9.8	-9.3	2.7	1.9	8.4	8.4	5.3	22.3	14.8	-2.3	-27.1	-29.8	2.4	36.3	18.5	16.0
All other transportation related commodities	8.4	7.3	4.5	7.8	-9.9	7.5	18.2	4.2	20.2	10.1	9.9	21.2	-49.0	-18.8	7.2	26.7	5.4	10.9	-10.9
Food services and drinking places	3.1	3.1	3.7	4.5	3.5	4.1	3.4	5.0	4.0	4.0	4.4	5.9	5.1	3.5	2.3	1.1	1.5	0.6	1.0
Recreation, entertainment, and shopping	2.5	2.5	2.3	3.6	1.6	3.3	2.4	1.3	3.7	4.1	4.5	6.4	-0.6	1.0	0.3	2.6	0.2	0.6	0.9
Recreation and entertain-nment	3.4	3.3	2.6	3.2	0.9	3.3	3.2	0.2	4.0	3.4	3.9	6.2	-1.8	0.5	-2.4	4.8	-0.2	-1.2	2.2
Shopping	1.5	1.8	2.1	3.9	2.1	3.3	1.8	2.2	3.4	4.6	5.0	6.5	0.2	1.3	2.3	1.0	0.5	1.9	-0.1
All tourism goods and services	4.8	4.5	3.4	5.0	-3.9	4.4	7.2	5.1	7.0	5.1	6.2	10.8	-15.9	-10.6	-3.7	6.1	6.5	4.1	2.7

Source: U.S. Bureau of Economic Analysis

Table 1.d. Chain-Type Price Indexes for Direct Tourism Output [Index numbers, 2000=100]

Tourism Goods and Services Group	2005	2006	2007	2008	2009	Seasonally adjusted at annual rates													
						Q2007:I	Q2007:II	Q2007:III	Q2007:IV	Q2008:I	Q2008:II	Q2008:III	Q2008:IV	Q2009:I	Q2009:II	Q2009:III	Q2009:IV	Q2010:I	Q2010:II
Traveler accommodations	114.8	119.1	124.8	125.0	116.6	121.7	124.2	127.0	126.1	126.4	124.3	125.8	123.6	118.6	116.6	115.2	116.1	114.2	119.2
Transportation	109.8	117.4	121.5	131.8	119.1	117.1	120.3	122.0	126.5	129.1	133.5	139.4	125.1	117.6	115.1	119.8	124.2	128.2	127.7
Passenger air transportation	96.6	102.8	104.6	114.8	104.2	102.7	103.2	105.3	107.4	108.8	114.4	118.4	117.7	108.8	99.6	100.2	108.2	112.9	117.2
All other transportation related commodities	120.1	128.8	134.6	145.1	130.8	128.2	133.7	135.1	141.5	144.9	148.4	155.6	131.6	124.9	127.0	134.8	136.6	140.2	136.2
Food services and drinking places	115.0	118.6	122.9	128.4	132.9	121.1	122.2	123.6	124.9	126.1	127.5	129.3	130.9	132.0	132.8	133.2	133.7	133.8	134.2
Recreation, entertainment, and shopping	113.0	115.7	118.4	122.7	124.7	117.5	118.2	118.5	119.6	120.8	122.2	124.1	123.9	124.2	124.3	125.1	125.1	125.3	125.6
Recreation and enterta-inment	114.0	117.7	120.8	124.7	125.8	119.8	120.7	120.8	122.0	123.0	124.2	126.1	125.5	125.6	124.9	126.4	126.3	125.9	126.6
Shopping	106.5	108.4	110.7	115.1	117.5	109.8	110.3	110.9	111.9	113.1	114.5	116.3	116.4	116.8	117.5	117.7	117.9	118.5	118.4
All tourism goods and services	111.5	116.5	120.5	126.6	121.7	117.7	119.8	121.3	123.3	124.9	126.8	130.1	124.6	121.2	120.0	121.8	123.7	125.0	125.8

Source: U.S. Bureau of Economic Analysis

Table 2. Direct Tourism Output[Millions of dollars]

Tourism Goods and Services Group	2005	2006	2007	2008	2009	Seasonally adjusted at annual rates													
						2007 -Q.I	2007 -Q.II	2007 -Q.III	2007 -Q.IV	2008 -Q.I	2008 -Q.II	2008 -Q.III	2008 -Q.IV	2009 -Q.I	2009 -Q.II	2009 -Q.III	2009 -Q.IV	2010 -Q.I	2010 -Q.II
Traveler accommodations	115,253	124,405	134,400	136,813	119,747	130,370	133,258	135,820	138,151	135,200	139,028	139,625	133,-399	120,-420	117,884	121,116	119,569	121,377	128,657
Transportation	253,000	274,823	287,334	301,483	259,154	276,777	287,451	293,379	291,729	304,293	311,213	313,628	276,797	250,-095	247,111	265,653	273,757	283,911	286,970
Passenger air transportation	98,162	105,101	109,203	111,545	93,452	106,386	110,293	113,249	106,884	113,692	113,793	110,911	107,-785	93,—754	88,019	93,539	98,497	103,787	108,753
All other transportation related commodities	154,840	169,739	178,156	189,993	165,773	170,404	177,173	180,138	184,909	190,-646	197,490	202,-824	169,-011	156,-375	159,170	172,209	175,337	180,187	178,245
Food services and drinking places	110,389	117,974	123,440	128,329	129,449	121,082	122,679	124,309	125,691	126,547	129,143	129,-005	128,-623	129,994	129,828	128,795	129,177	131,552	132,605
Recreation, entertainment, and shopping	181,418	192,490	197,082	200,496	199,930	196,127	196,509	197,517	198,176	198,904	202,748	202,391	197,94 1	199,477	198,861	199,854	201,527	203,481	202,679
Recreation and entertainment	78,265	82,445	85,162	85,314	85,219	84,734	84,922	85,567	85,425	84,788	85,899	85,—772	84,796	85,552	84,954	85,161	85,209	85,263	84,085
Shopping	103,155	110,045	111,922	115,181	114,-710	111,395	111,589	111,952	112,752	114,116	116,846	116,617	113,145	113,-926	113,906	114,692	116,316	118,214	118,588
All tourism goods and services	660,053	709,678	742,237	767,100	708,309	724,344	739,877	751,001	753,727	764,918	782,103	784,617	736,-761	700,-023	693,725	715,440	724,048	740,335	750,918
Percent change at annual rate	7.8	7.5	4.6	3.3	7.7	4.1	8.9	6.2	1.5	6.1	9.3	1.3	22.3	-18.5	3.6	13.1	4.9	9.3	5.8

Source: U.S. Bureau of Economic Analysis

Table 3. Total Tourism-Related Output[Millions of dollars]

Tourism Goods and Services Group	2005	2006	2007	2008	2009	Seasonally adjusted at annual rates													
						Q2007:I	Q2007:II	Q2007:III	Q2007:IV	Q2008:I	Q2008:II	Q2008:III	Q2008:IV	Q2009:I	Q2009:II	Q2009:III	Q2009:IV	Q2010:I	Q2010:II
Traveler accommodations	177,575	191,675	207,075	210,793	184,499	200,866	205,316	209,263	212,855	208,309	214,206	215,125	205,534	185,536	181,628	186,608	184,225	187,011	198,227
Transportation	435,460	473,728	495,580	520,699	445,851	476,872	495,897	505,874	503,679	525,881	538,017	542,642	476,256	429,585	424,762	457,382	471,675	489,470	493,908
Passenger air transportation	166,506	178,276	185,234	189,207	158,517	180,455	187,083	192,097	181,301	192,849	193,020	188,130	182,828	159,028	149,301	158,664	167,074	176,048	184,471
All other transportation related commodities	268,960	295,487	310,395	331,596	287,457	296,442	308,845	313,796	322,495	333,120	345,129	354,708	293,427	270,613	275,595	298,883	304,737	313,537	309,487
Food services and drinking places	207,522	221,780	232,056	241,247	243,351	227,624	230,625	233,690	236,287	237,896	242,776	242,517	241,799	244,376	244,065	242,122	242,841	247,306	249,285
Recreation, entertainment, and shopping	343,093	364,240	372,574	379,644	378,679	370,777	371,497	373,306	374,715	376,561	384,063	383,336	374,614	377,557	376,582	378,522	382,054	386,056	384,877
Recreation and entertainment	129,006	135,846	140,294	140,583	140,599	139,591	139,907	140,967	140,709	139,714	141,542	141,291	139,786	141,111	140,173	140,480	140,632	140,686	138,719
Shopping	214,094	228,395	232,290	239,054	238,076	231,195	231,599	232,352	234,013	236,842	242,510	242,034	234,828	236,449	236,407	238,038	241,409	245,347	246,125
All tourism goods and services	1,163,628	1,251,382	1,307,275	1,352,316	1,252,392	1,276,151	1,303,310	1,322,101	1,327,536	1,348,545	1,378,963	1,383,511	1,298,244	1,237,125	1,227,099	1,264,623	1,280,722	1,309,732	1,326,242
Percent change at annual rate	7.7	7.5	4.5	3.4	-7.4	4.1	8.8	5.9	1.7	6.5	9.3	1.3	22.5	17.5	-3.2	12.8	5.2	9.4	5.1

Source: U.S. Bureau of Economic Analysis

Table 4. Percent Change in Direct Tourism Employment[Percent change from preceding period]

Tourism Industry Group	2005	2006	2007	2008	2009	Seasonally adjusted at annual rates													
						Q-2007:-I	Q-2007:-II	Q-2007:-III	Q-2007:-IV	Q-2008:-I	Q-2008:--II	Q-2008-III	Q-2008:-IV	Q-2009--I	Q-2009-II	Q-2009:-III	Q-2009:-IV	Q-2010:-I	Q-2010:-II
Traveler accommodations	1.3	0.4	1.0	0.0	-5.7	0.0	0.0	0.2	4.3	0.5	-1.1	-3.6	-4.1	-9.2	-8.3	-2.9	-2.0	-0.1	4.7
Transportation	-0.5	0.6	1.2	-0.1	-6.5	0.5	1.4	1.5	3.1	1.9	-2.0	-4.4	-6.8	-9.8	-7.7	-4.1	-2.5	-2.0	2.5
Air -transportation services	-3.1	-1.2	1.0	0.5	-5.8	-0.8	2.7	1.5	4.1	4.5	-2.4	-5.8	-7.5	-7.0	-5.7	-4.5	-2.2	-2.0	0.5
All other transportation related industries	1.3	1.8	1.3	-0.5	-7.0	1.4	0.6	1.5	2.5	0.1	-1.7	-3.5	-6.3	-11.6	-9.0	-3.8	-2.8	-2.0	4.0
Food services and drinking places	4.7	2.6	1.7	0.2	-2.3	1.9	0.5	1.4	2.0	0.5	-0.8	-1.3	-3.2	-3.9	-1.0	-1.7	-2.1	-0.9	1.0
Recreation, entertainment, and shopping	-0.7	0.8	-0.1	-0.3	-3.7	-0.7	-0.9	-0.3	2.3	1.0	-1.8	-2.0	-3.8	-6.9	-3.3	-0.3	-3.4	-2.3	1.4
Recreation and entertainment	1.7	1.0	2.2	1.2	-2.3	4.2	0.3	1.1	4.4	2.6	-1.0	-1.3	-1.8	-5.8	-1.7	2.6	-4.1	-4.0	1.8
Shopping	-3.3	0.6	-2.7	-1.9	-5.4	-6.0	-2.4	-1.9	-0.2	-0.9	-2.9	-2.7	-6.2	-8.3	-5.2	-3.7	-2.5	-0.1	0.8
All other industries	0.3	4.0	1.7	-0.7	-6.3	0.0	1.4	0.8	1.6	-1.3	-1.7	-2.2	-4.3	-10.3	-9.1	-5.5	-1.9	-1.1	1.1
All tourism industries	1.5	1.4	1.0	0.0	-4.4	0.6	0.3	0.8	2.8	0.8	-1.4	-2.6	-4.3	-7.2	-4.8	-2.3	-2.4	-1.2	2.2

Source: U.S. Bureau of Economic Analysis

Table 5. Direct Tourism Employment[Thousands]

Tourism Industry Group	2005	2006	2007	2008	2009	Seasonally adjusted at annual rates													
						Q-2007:I	Q-2007:II	Q-2007:III	Q-2007:IV	Q-2008:I	Q-2008:II	Q-2008:III	Q-2008:IV	Q-2009:I	Q-2009:II	Q-2009:III	Q-2009:IV	Q-2010:I	Q-2010:II
Traveler accommodations	1,357.8	1,362.8	1,375.8	1,375.8	1,297.5	1,371.9	1,371.8	1,372.5	1,387.1	1,388.8	1,384.7	1,372.0	1,357.6	1,325.3	1,296.8	1,287.2	1,280.6	1,280.2	1,295.0
Transportation	1,111.0	1,117.3	1,130.5	1,129.8	1,055.9	1,123.2	1,127.2	1,131.4	1,140.2	1,145.5	1,139.7	1,126.9	1,17.3	1,079.1	1,057.7	1,046.7	1,040.0	1,034.8	1,041.3
Air transportation services	452.4	447.0	451.6	454.0	427.5	447.4	450.3	452.0	456.6	461.7	458.9	452.1	443.4	435.3	429.0	424.1	421.7	419.6	420.1
All other transportation related industries	658.5	670.4	679.0	675.9	628.4	675.9	676.9	679.4	683.6	683.8	680.9	674.8	663.9	643.8	628.8	622.7	618.3	615.2	621.2
Food -services and drinking places	1,859.2	1,908.3	1,939.9	1,943.6	1,898.7	1,932.2	1,934.6	1,9-41.4	1,951.2	1,9-53.5	1,94-9.8	1,9-43.6	1,92-7.6	1,90-8.7	1,90-4.1	1,89-5.8	1,88-6.0	1,8-81.8	1,8-86.5
Recreation, entertainment, and shopping	1,189.1	1,198.7	1,197.7	1,194.6	1,150.7	1,198.5	1,195.7	1,19-4.9	1,201.7	1,204.6	1,1-99.1	1,19-3.2	1,1-81.7	1,16-0.7	1,151.1	1,15-0.4	1,14-0.6	1,1-33.9	1,13-7.7
Recreation and entertain-ment	630.1	636.6	650.8	658.3	643.2	647.7	648.2	650.0	657.1	66---1.3	65---9.7	657.5	654.6	64---4.9	64---2.1	64---6.2	63---9.5	63---3.0	63---5.8
Shopping	559.0	562.2	547.0	536.4	507.6	550.9	547.5	544.9	544.6	543.4	539.4	535.7	527.2	515.9	509.1	504.3	501.2	501.0	502.0
All other industries	249.6	259.6	264.1	262.3	245.7	262.9	263.8	264.4	265.4	264.6	263.4	262.0	259.1	252.2	246.2	242.8	241.6	240.9	241.6
All tourism industries	5,766.6	5,846.8	5,908.1	5,906.2	5,648.5	5,888.8	5,893.3	5,904.6	5,945.6	5,956.9	5,936.7	5,897.6	5,833.4	5,726.1	5,656.0	5,623.0	5,588.9	5,571.7	5,602.2

Source: U.S. Bureau of Economic Analysis

Table 6. Total Tourism-Related Employment [Thousands]

Tourism Industry Group	2005	2006	2007	2008	2009	Seasonally adjusted at annual rates													
						Q-2007:-I	Q-2007:-I	Q-2007:-III	Q-2007-IV	Q-2008:-I	Q-2008:-II	Q-2008:-III	Q-2008:-IV	Q-2009:-I	Q-2009:-II	Q-2009:-III	Q-2009:-IV	Q-2010:-I	Q-2010:-II
Traveler accommodations	1,687.1	1,694.3	1,712.4	1,712.0	1,614.6	1,707.2	1,707.4	1,708.5	1,726.6	1,728.2	1,723.2	1,707.2	1,689.3	1,649.3	1,613.8	1,601.7	1,593.5	1,593.0	1,611.1
Transportation	1,954.9	1,968.3	1,989.9	1,990.6	1,855.5	1,977.4	1,901.	1,991.3	2,006.7	2,017.4	2,007.9	1,985.5	1,951.6	1,899.2	1,859.8	1,837.8	1,825.3	1,816.1	1,827.4
Air transportation services	801.7	792.0	800.2	804.5	757.6	792.7	798.0	801.0	809.2	818.1	813.1	801.1	785.6	771.4	760.2	751.4	747.3	743.5	744.4
All other transportation related industries	1,153.2	1,176.4	1,189.8	1,186.2	1,098.0	1,184.8	1,186.2	1,190.4	1,197.7	1,199.4	1,194.8	1,184.5	1,166.1	1,127.9	1,099.7	1,086.4	1,078.1	1,072.6	1,083.0
Food services and drinking places	2,486.2	2,551.9	2,594.1	2,599.2	2,539.0	2,583.9	2,587.1	2,596.2	2,609.2	2,612.4	2,607.4	2,599.1	2,577.8	2,552.5	2,546.3	2,535.2	2,522.1	2,516.4	2,522.7
Recreation, entertainment, and shopping	1,864.5	1,873.2	1,864.5	1,856.7	1,784.7	1,867.4	1,861.9	1,859.8	1,868.8	1,872.2	1,863.3	1,853.9	1,837.2	1,802.7	1,785.7	1,782.6	1,767.9	1,756.1	1,763.4
Recreation and entertainment	925.1	932.9	952.1	962.7	940.9	948.0	948.6	951.1	960.9	967.0	964.7	961.4	957.5	943.3	939.3	945.0	936.1	926.3	931.6
Shopping	939.4	940.4	912.4	894.1	843.9	919.5	913.3	908.8	908.0	905.3	898.7	892.6	879.9	859.5	846.5	837.7	832.0	829.9	831.9
All other industries	422.6	439.1	447.1	444.2	416.6	444.8	446.6	447.5	449.3	448.0	446.2	443.7	438.8	427.4	417.4	411.7	409.8	408.7	409.9
All tourism industries	8,415.4	8,526.8	8,608.0	8,602.7	8,210.6	8,580.7	8,587.1	8,603.4	8,660.7	8,678.3	8,647.9	8,589.5	8,494.9	8,331.2	8,223.3	8,169.2	8,118.9	8,090.6	8,134.7
Percent change at annual rate	*1.5*	*1.3*	*1.0*	*-0.1*	*-4.6*	*0.5*	*0.3*	*0.8*	*2.7*	*0.8*	*-1.4*	*-2.7*	*-4.3*	*-7.5*	*-5.1*	*-2.6*	*-2.4*	*-1.4*	*2.2*

Source: U.S. Bureau of Economic Analysis

In: United States Travel and Tourism Industry   ISBN: 978-1-61209-111-2
Editors: D.P. Moore and A.G. Doherty   © 2011 Nova Science Publishers, Inc.

Chapter 3

INTERNATIONAL VISITATION TO THE UNITED STATES: A STATISTICAL SUMMARY OF U.S. ARRIVALS (2009)[*]

U.S. Dept. of Commerce

WHY IS INTERNATIONAL TRAVEL IMPORTANT?

- The United States is the number two destination for global international travel.
- International travel and tourism accounts for approximately four percent of total travelers within the United States.
- But where it counts – "total spending, employment, payroll and taxes" - the international travel share is about ten percentage points higher, roughly 14 percent of all U.S. travel.
- International travelers support an estimated 1.1 million jobs and generate about $17 billion in federal, state and local taxes

---

[*] This is an edited, reformatted and augmented edition of a United States Department of Commerce Internatonal Trade Adminstration Manufacturing ans Services, dated 2009.

U.S. TRAVEL & TOURISM: INTERNATIONAL VISITATION TO THE UNITED STATES 2009

After two straight years of record international visitation to the United States, in 2009 visits dropped as the global economic downturn slowed travel around the world. The top inbound markets continued to be Canada and Mexico, both of which were down in arrivals along with six of the nine overseas regional markets. South America, Asia and Oceania experienced the strongest growth in the fourth quarter, due in part to increases from the emerging markets of China and Brazil. During the fourth quarter total arrivals increased two percent. That marked the first quarter to experience growth in 2009. Positive growth occurred in 15 of the top 20 arrival markets. Arrivals from overseas, Canada and Mexico were up one percent, four percent and three percent, respectively.

Annual overseas arrivals (excluding Canada and Mexico) totaled 23.8 million during 2009, down six percent from 2008. Travel from overseas markets accounted for 43 percent of total arrivals to the United States. While overseas travel was still down 9 percent from its peak in 2000, visitation from overseas markets is up 32 percent from its low in 2003. Five of the top 50 overseas markets set new visitation records: Australia, China/PRC, Colombia, Ecuador and Panama.

In 2009, seven of the top 20 arrival markets posted increases, with Brazil and Argentina accounting for double-digit increases. The United Kingdom and Japan were among thirteen markets which experienced declines for the year. The top 20 inbound visitor mar-kets accounted for 89 percent of all international arrivals to the United States dur-ing 2009 and as a group it was down six percent compared to 2008.

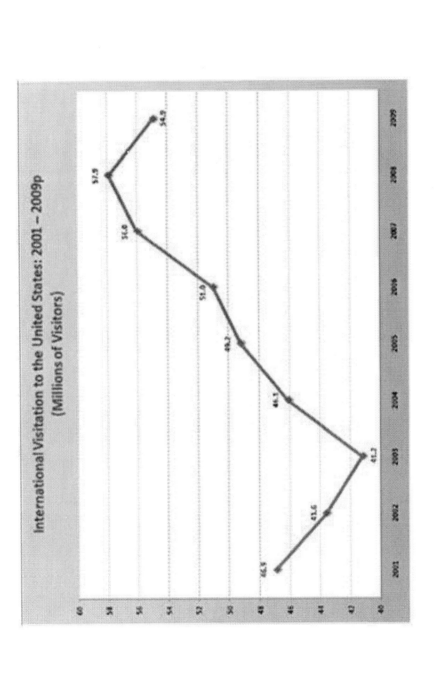

International Visitation to the United States: 2001 – 2009p
(Millions of Visitors)

International Visitors (Inbound) and U.S. Residents (Outbound) International Travelers to/from the United States 2001 - 2009ᵖ

International Visitors (Inbound)	2001	2002	2003	2004	2005	2006	2007	2008	2009ᵖ
Total Inbound (000s)	46,927	43,581	41,218	46,086	49,206	50,977	55,979	57,937	54,884
% Change	-8%	-7%	-5%	12%	7%	4%	10%	3%	-5%
Overseas¹	21,833	19,117	18,026	20,322	21,679	21,668	23,892	25,341	23,756
% Change	-16%	-12%	-6%	13%	7%	0%	10%	6%	-6%
Canada	13,527	13,024	12,666	13,857	14,862	15,992	17,760	18,910	17,964
% Change	-8%	-4%	-3%	9%	7%	8%	11%	6%	-5%
Mexico	11,567	11,440	10,526	11,907	12,665	13,317	14,327	13,686	13,164
% Change	9%	-1%	-8%	13%	6%	5%	8%	-4%	-4%
U.S. Residents (Outbound)	**2001**	**2002**	**2003**	**2004**	**2005**	**2006**	**2007**	**2008**	**2009ᵖ**
Total Outbound (000s)	59,442	58,065	56,250	61,809	63,503	63,662	64,028	63,684	na
% Change	-3%	-2%	-3%	10%	3%	0%	1%	-1%	
Overseas	25,249	23,397	24,452	27,351	28,787	30,148	31,228	30,789	na
% Change	-6%	-7%	5%	12%	5%	5%	4%	-1%	
Canada	15,570	16,167	14,232	15,088	14,391	13,855	13,375	12,504	na
% Change	3%	4%	-12%	6%	-5%	-4%	-3%	-7%	
Mexico	18,623	18,501	17,566	19,370	20,325	19,659	19,425	20,391	na
% Change	-3%	-1%	-5%	10%	5%	-3%	-1%	5%	

Sources: U.S. Department of Commerce, ITA, Office of Travel & Tourism Industries; Statistics Canada and Banco de Mexico/Secretaria de Turismo.

¹ Overseas excludes Canada and Mexico.

p = Preliminary. Released: March 2010.

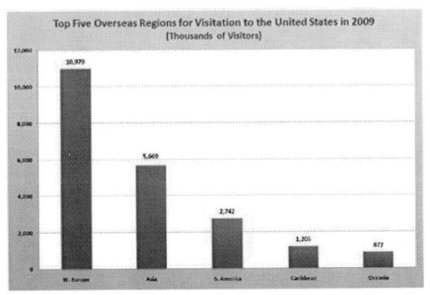

Source: U.S. Department of Commerce, ITA, Office of Travel & Tourism Industries
Released: March 2010.

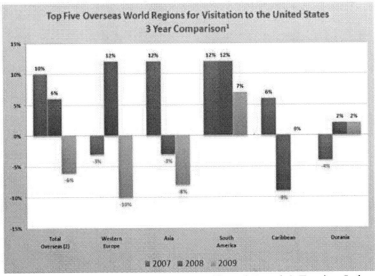

Source: U.S. Department of Commerce, ITA, Office of Travel & Tourism Industries.
(1) The percent change was calculated by comparing the yearly data to the previous
    year's data.
(2) "Overseas" excludes Canada and Mexico.
Released: March 2010.

International Visitors to the U.S. by Region of Residency
2008 vs 2009[p]

Region/Country of Residence	2008	2009[p]	% Change (2009/2008)
Total Arrivals[1]	57,937,451	54,884,184	-5%
North America[2]	32,673,000	31,128,000	-5%
Canada[3]	18,910,000	17,964,000	-5%
Canada Air[3]	6,348,000	6,091,000	-4%
Mexico[3]	13,686,000	13,164,000	-4%
Mexico Air[4]	1,708,320	1,511,110	-12%
Overseas[5]	25,341,451	23,756,184	-6%
Western Europe	12,198,081	10,978,668	-10%
Asia	6,178,602	5,668,721	-8%
South America	2,555,599	2,741,535	7%
Caribbean	1,201,149	1,206,068	0%
Oceania	851,619	871,982	2%
Central America	775,590	757,905	-2%
Middle East	680,974	665,942	-2%
Eastern Europe	584,602	571,598	-2%
Africa	315,235	293,765	-7%

Sources: U.S. Department of Commerce, ITA, Office of Travel & Tourism Industries: Statistics Canada and Banco de Mexico/Secretaria de Turismo.

(p) Preliminary

(1) Total Arrivals is the sum of Canada, Mexico and all Overseas.

(2) North America includes Canada and Mexico only.

(3) Figures are based on survey data obtained from their respective governments and therefore rounded to the nearest thousand.

(4) Mexico air data are based on the Department of Homeland Security I-94 form.

(5) "Overseas" excludes Canada and Mexico

Top 50 Markets for International Visitors to the United States
2008 vs 2009[p]

Rank	Region/Country of Residence	2008	2009[p]	% Change (2009/2008)
	Total Arrivals[1]	57,937,451	54,884,184	-5%
	North America[2]	32,673,000	31,128,000	-5%
1	Canada[3]	18,910,000	17,964,000	-5%
	Canada Air[3]	6,348,000	6,091,000	-4%
2	Mexico[3]	13,686,000	13,164,000	-4%
	Mexico Air[4]	1,708,320	1,511,110	-12%
	Overseas[5]	25,341,451	23,756,184	-6%

Table (Continued)

Rank	Region/Country of Residence	2008	2009ᵖ	% Change (2009/2008)
3	United Kingdom	4,564,895	3,899,167	-15%
4	Japan	3,249,578	2,918,268	-10%
5	Germany	1,782,299	1,686,825	-5%
6	France	1,243,942	1,204,490	-3%
7	Brazil	769,232	892,611	16%
8	Italy	779,463	753,310	-3%
9	South Korea	759,394	743,846	-2%
10	Australia	689,927	723,576	5%
11	Spain	658,333	596,766	-9%
12	India	598,971	549,474	-8%
13	Netherlands	607,802	547,790	-10%
14	China, PRC	492,958	524,817	6%
15	Venezuela	507,153	507,185	0%
16	Colombia	419,268	424,526	1%
17	Ireland	531,198	411,203	-23%
18	Argentina	318,144	356,428	12%
19	Switzerland	341,955	355,727	4%
20	Sweden	397,017	324,417	-18%
21	Israel	332,257	308,213	-7%
22	Belgium	265,383	245,710	-7%
23	Denmark	256,604	245,623	-4%
24	Taiwan	294,893	239,545	-19%
25	Dominican Republic	226,184	227,948	1%
26	Bahamas	180,914	224,812	24%
27	Norway	213,983	193,318	-10%
28	Guatemala	188,177	189,455	1%
29	Jamaica	204,982	185,526	-9%
30	Philippines	179,820	171,680	-5%
31	Ecuador	152,112	168,432	11%
32	Austria	158,764	162,569	2%
33	Peru	162,883	160,474	-1%
34	Costa Rica	165,257	157,471	-5%
35	Russia	142,998	142,650	0%
36	Trinidad and Tobago	147,613	141,406	-4%
37	New Zealand	145,325	131,012	-10%
38	Chile	130,813	126,609	-3%
39	El Salvador	136,494	123,185	-10%
40	Hong Kong	139,359	116,023	-17%
41	Honduras	116,902	115,405	-1%
42	Poland	146,887	115,327	-21%

Table (Continued)

Rank	Region/Country of Residence	2008	2009ᴾ	% Change (2009/2008)
43	Finland	118,448	114,364	-3%
44	Panama	102,832	109,968	7%
45	Singapore	141,474	107,400	-24%
46	Turkey	107,572	94,302	-12%
47	Haiti	91,748	80,572	-12%
48	South Africa	93,692	78,934	-16%
49	Portugal	89,158	74,457	-16%
50	Thailand	76,820	69,204	-10%

Sources: U.S. Department of Commerce, ITA, Office of Travel & Tourism Industries:
   Statistics Canada and Banco de Mexico/Secretaria de Turismo.
(p) Preliminary.
(1) Total Arrivals is the sum of Canada, Mexico and all Overseas.
(2) North America includes Canada and Mexico only.
(3) Figures are based on survey data obtained from their respective governments and
   therefore rounded to the nearest thousand.
(4) Mexico air data are based on the Department of Homeland Security I-94 form.
(5) "Overseas" excludes Canada and Mexico.

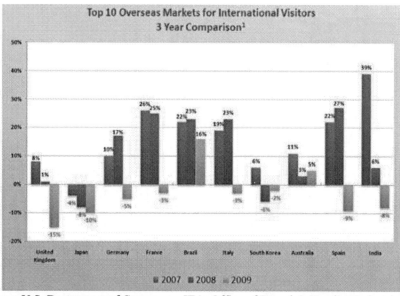

Source: U.S. Department of Commerce, ITA, Office of Travel & Tourism Industries.
(1) The percent change was calculated by comparing the yearly data to the previous
   year's data.
Released: March 2010.

International Visitors to United States: Country of Residency Historical Arrivals 2001 - 2009^P
(Top 50 Origin Countries)

Rank	Country of Residence	2001	2002	2003	2004	2005	2006	2007	2008	2009^P
	Total Visitation	46,926,868	43,580,707	41,218,213	46,086,257	49,205,528	50,977,290	55,979,277	57,937,451	54,884,184
1	Canada	13,527,000	13,024,000	12,666,000	13,857,000	14,862,000	15,992,000	17,760,000	18,910,000	17,964,000
2	Mexico	11,567,000	11,440,000	10,526,000	11,907,000	12,665,000	13,317,000	14,327,000	13,686,000	13,164,000
3	United Kingdom	4,097,258	3,816,736	3,936,112	4,302,737	4,344,957	4,176,211	4,497,858	4,564,895	3,899,167
4	Japan	4,082,661	3,627,264	3,169,682	3,747,620	3,883,906	3,672,584	3,531,489	3,249,578	2,918,268
5	Germany	1,313,756	1,189,856	1,180,212	1,319,904	1,415,530	1,385,520	1,524,151	1,782,299	1,686,825
6	France	875,854	734,260	688,887	775,274	878,648	789,815	997,506	1,243,942	1,204,490
7	Brazil	551,406	405,094	348,945	384,734	485,373	525,271	639,431	769,232	892,611
8	Italy	472,348	406,160	408,633	470,805	545,546	532,829	634,152	779,463	753,310
9	South Korea	617,892	638,697	617,573	626,595	705,093	757,721	806,175	759,394	743,846
10	Australia	425,934	407,130	405,698	519,955	581,773	603,275	669,536	689,927	723,576
11	Spain	291,052	269,520	284,031	333,432	385,640	424,224	516,471	658,333	596,766
12	India	269,674	257,271	272,161	308,845	344,926	406,845	567,045	598,971	549,474
13	Netherlands	411,742	384,367	373,690	424,872	448,650	446,785	506,852	607,802	547,790
14	China (PRC)	232,416	225,565	157,326	202,544	270,272	320,450	397,405	492,958	524,817
15	Venezuela	555,292	395,913	284,423	330,285	340,315	369,037	458,678	507,153	507,185
16	Colombia	371,747	321,439	280,259	295,371	325,398	348,388	389,752	419,268	424,526
17	Ireland	276,806	259,687	254,320	345,119	383,400	414,423	491,055	531,198	411,203
18	Argentina	434,011	164,658	150,719	167,726	188,865	212,096	266,971	318,144	356,428
19	Switzerland	310,826	253,940	230,042	243,186	256,730	270,571	296,369	341,955	355,727
20	Sweden	230,538	204,156	211,386	254,258	290,530	285,994	337,474	397,017	324,417

Table (Continued)

Rank	Country of Residence	2001	2002	2003	2004	2005	2006	2007	2008	2009ᴾ
21	Israel	305,431	263,097	249,034	275,373	284,310	283,889	313,077	332,257	308,213
22	Belgium	181,693	159,052	151,069	175,997	191,596	188,311	216,579	265,383	245,710
23	Denmark	126,345	118,716	125,435	150,839	174,581	185,337	217,593	256,604	245,623
24	Taiwan	357,064	288,032	238,999	297,684	318,886	300,382	311,020	294,893	239,545
25	Dominican Republic	171,568	153,586	153,019	180,048	221,449	236,622	263,452	226,184	227,948
26	Bahamas	293,022	262,469	253,229	265,681	237,140	243,300	256,433	180,914	224,812
27	Norway	123,268	112,593	113,233	130,400	139,043	145,359	172,882	213,983	193,318
28	Guatemala	171,955	162,367	151,891	161,983	170,076	173,793	201,286	188,177	189,455
29	Jamaica	229,003	183,903	159,484	163,059	175,351	204,912	221,521	204,982	185,526
30	Philippines	180,549	173,203	134,338	143,962	153,821	153,887	171,829	179,820	171,680
31	Ecuador	147,527	139,094	119,737	133,046	143,073	147,173	155,328	152,112	168,432
32	Austria	123,295	97,930	99,924	112,950	117,688	117,191	131,339	158,764	162,569
33	Peru	186,008	164,482	154,324	151,409	151,823	133,398	148,967	162,883	160,474
34	Costa Rica	143,434	124,993	112,880	127,112	133,820	130,702	160,444	165,257	157,471
35	Russia	70,348	64,228	62,330	72,419	84,780	94,681	114,850	142,998	142,650
36	Trindad & Tobago	127,102	118,336	111,820	121,158	128,392	133,906	143,009	147,613	141,406
37	New Zealand	144,216	109,580	107,214	127,394	139,780	138,486	147,735	145,325	131,012
38	Chile	150,350	115,359	95,389	101,171	101,550	110,143	123,152	130,813	126,609
39	El Salvador	207,890	197,159	177,240	181,209	164,492	153,835	159,783	136,494	123,185
40	Hong Kong	170,267	135,409	114,112	123,335	135,108	137,278	142,419	139,359	116,023
41	Honduras	87,645	85,322	82,099	85,506	89,718	92,445	111,059	116,902	115,405
42	Poland	108,244	108,707	107,892	123,003	134,430	137,588	138,525	146,887	115,327
43	Finland	72,864	64,860	67,761	78,612	89,125	87,904	96,173	118,448	114,364
44	Panama	87,714	75,495	72,413	76,032	78,855	81,358	87,329	102,832	109,968

Table (Continued)

Rank	Country of Residence	2001	2002	2003	2004	2005	2006	2007	2008	2009[p]
45	Singapore	99,010	97,259	87,525	106,527	115,939	122,995	135,209	141,474	107,400
46	Turkey	82,222	78,662	75,227	76,404	84,434	90,122	95,568	107,572	94,302
47	Haiti	65,169	59,444	59,756	60,521	63,970	58,918	83,837	91,748	80,572
48	South Africa	94,882	73,910	72,029	78,433	89,102	89,017	93,719	93,692	78,934
49	Portugal	67,222	56,012	54,572	60,930	68,111	71,406	80,611	89,158	74,457
50	Thailand	73,745	66,848	55,884	66,287	66,833	69,236	77,009	76,820	69,204

Sources: U.S. Department of Commerce, ITA, Manufacturing & Services, Office of Travel & Tourism Industries; Statistics Canada and Banco de Mexico/Secretaria de Turismo.

(p) Preliminary

Released: March 2010.

Visitation to the United States: Pleasure Travel[1] vs. Business Travel from Top Overseas Countries Sending Pleasure Travelers to the United States January - December 2009

Country of Residence	Percent Change Pleasure Travelers	Pleasure Arrivals Rank	Percent Change Business Travelers	Total Arrivals	Percent Change Total Arrivals	Total Arrivals Rank	Pleasure Travel Percent of Total	Business Travel Percent of Total
United Kingdom	-14	1	-20	3,899,152	-15	1	87.5%	12.2%
Japan	-7	2	-32	2,918,264	-10	2	89.8%	8.8%
Germany	-1	3	-23	1,686,825	-5	3	83.0%	16.1%
France	1	4	-22	1,204,489	-3	4	85.6%	13.4%
Brazil	25	5	-19	892,604	16	5	85.6%	12.7%
Italy	-1	6	-18	753,308	-3	6	86.3%	12.7%

Table (Continued)

Country of Residence	Percent Change Pleasure Travelers	Pleasure Arrivals Rank	Percent Change Business Travelers	Total Arrivals	Percent Change Total Arrivals	Total Arrivals Rank	Pleasure Travel Percent of Total	Business Travel Percent of Total
Australia	9	7	-17	723,571	5	8	86.2%	13.3%
Spain	-9	8	-17	596,762	-9	9	88.8%	9.8%
South Korea	5	9	-18	743,843	-2	7	68.2%	18.1%
Venezuela	3	10	-22	507,148	0	13	88.5%	9.9%
Netherlands	-7	11	-21	547,789	-10	11	81.9%	17.6%
Ireland	-24	12	-9	411,202	-23	15	90.8%	8.8%
Colombia	4	13	-11	424,332	1	14	83.9%	14.1%
India	-1	14	-22	549,212	-8	10	63.3%	25.0%
Argentina	20	15	-19	356,426	12	16	85.8%	13.5%
Total Overseas[2] Arrivals	-4		-20	23,756,005	-6		82.4%	14.6%

Source: U.S. Department of Commerce, ITA, Manufacturing & Services, Office of Travel & Tourism Industries

(1). The monthly figures on all travelers from each country to the United States represent mainly business, pleasure and student travelers. For some countries, there is a significant difference in the rate of change by the type of visa. The table above shows these differences for the top 15 overseas tourist-generating countries, specifically the change in pleasure travel versus business travel.

(2). "Overseas" excludes Canada and Mexico, but includes all visitor visa types. Released: March 2010.

Top 15 Ports-of-Entry for Overseas[1] Visitors
to the United States 2008 vs. 2009

Rank	Ports[2]	2008 Total Overseas	2009 Total Overseas	% Change 2009/2008	2009 Market Share	Cumulative Market Share
--	Grand Total	25,341,451	23,756,184	-6%	100.0%	--
1	New York, Ny	4,255,262	4,011,310	-6%	16.9%	16.9%
2	Miami, Fl	3,097,120	3,136,189	1%	13.2%	30.1%
3	Los Angeles, Ca	2,345,741	2,194,780	-6%	9.2%	39.3%
4	Newark, Nj	1,834,483	1,688,467	-8%	7.1%	46.4%
5	Honolulu, Hi	1,314,662	1,292,461	-2%	5.4%	51.9%
6	San Francisco, Ca	1,422,728	1,230,389	-14%	5.2%	57.1%
7	Chicago, Il	1,347,963	1,132,921	-16%	4.8%	61.8%
8	Atlanta, Ga	1,064,096	989,376	-7%	4.2%	66.0%
9	Agana, Gu	976,620	929,407	-5%	3.9%	69.9%
10	Washington, Dc	836,176	820,026	-2%	3.5%	73.4%
11	Orlando, Fl	708,337	791,894	12%	3.3%	76.7%
12	Houston, Tx	549,496	551,912	0%	2.3%	79.0%
13	Boston, Ma	532,013	502,624	-6%	2.1%	81.1%
14	Philadelphia, Pa	427,212	448,020	5%	1.9%	83.0%
15	Ft. Lauderdale, Fl	373,667	386,555	3%	1.6%	84.6%

Source: U.S. Department of Commerce, ITA, Manufacturing & Services, Office of
    Travel & Tourism Industries
(1) "Overseas" excludes Canada and Mexico.
(2) This is one column from a report containing 29 tables of international arrivals data.
    Forty ports of entry are tracked each month by world region and select countries.
Released: March 2010.

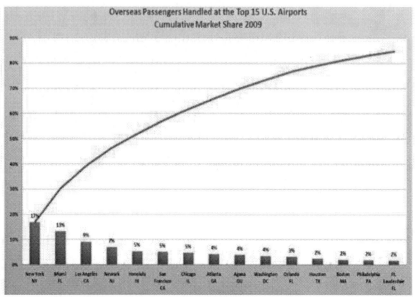

Source: U.S. Department of Commerce, ITA, Office of Travel & Tourism Industries

The data presented in this graph is from a report containing 29 tables of international arrivals data. Forty ports of entry are tracked each month by world and selected countries. ld region

Released: March 2010.

In: United States Travel and Tourism Industry   ISBN: 978-1-61209-111-2
Editors: D.P. Moore and A.G. Doherty   © 2011 Nova Science Publishers, Inc.

Chapter 4

TOP 10 INTERNATIONAL MARKETS: 2009 VISITATION AND SPENDING*

U.S. Dept. of Commerce

Top 10 Markets: 2009 International Visitation

Rank		Country	2009 Arrivals
1		**Canada (-5%)**	**17.96 Million**
		In 2009, Canada remained the leader in international arrivals to the United States, despite a 5% drop from 2008, finishing 1.1 million visitors away from their 1991 record of 19.1 million. This decline ended a five year span of at least 6% annual growth, but Canada still accounted for over 33% of the total international arrivals into the United States.	
2		**Mexico (-4%)**	**13.16 Million**
		Mexico carried their 2008 downturn into 2009 with a similar 4% decline in international arrivals to the United States. These declines equate to a difference of 1.16 million arrivals from their 2007 record of 14.3 million. Mexico accounted for a 24% share of 2009 visitor volume.	
3		**United Kingdom (-15%)**	**3.90 Million**
		The United Kingdom witnessed the largest drop in visitation rates among the top-10, with a 15% decline in 2009. This was due to a rough 1st quarter, with an especially bitter March that saw a near 31% drop in visitation from 2008. The United Kingdom accounted for a 7.1% share of 2009 visitor volume.	

---

* This is an edited, reformatted and augmented edition of a United States Department of Commerce Internatonal Trade Adminstration, dated 2009.

U.S. Dept. of Commerce

Table (Continued)

Rank		Country	2009 Arrivals
4		**Japan (-10%)**	**2.92 Million**
		Japan continued its slide in visitation that began 4 years ago, with a 10% drop in 2009. This year marks the lowest arrival numbers from Japan since 1988. Japan's 2009 drop prolongs a gradual decline of visitors, totaling 46%, since their record of 5.4 million visitors in 1997. Japan accounted for a 5.3% share of 2009 visitor volume.	
5		**Germany (-5%)**	**1.69 Million**
		After an excellent year in 2008, Germany posted a 5% loss in 2009, after recovering from double-digit declines in the first quarter. The 2009 visitation level is 300,000 visitors short of their record 2 million set in 1996. Germany accounted for a 3.1% share of 2009 visitor volume.	
6		**France (-3%)**	**1.20 Million**
		As the result of a rocky second-half in 2009, France fell 3% following up a record-setting year in 2008. The 1.2 million arrivals in 2009 still mark the second most arrivals from France in history. France accounted for a 2.2% share of 2009 visitor volume.	
7		**Brazil (+16%)**	**893,000**
		The only top-10 country to move up the rankings in 2009 was Brazil, riding a 16% surge in international arrivals coupled with a slight decline in Italian visitation. This extends a 5-year period in which the average increase in visitation was 18% annually. Since 2003, Brazil has more than doubled visitation (156%) to the United States. Brazil accounted for a 1.6% share of 2009 visitor volume.	
8		**Italy (-3%)**	**753,000**
		Italy followed up its record visitation year of 779,463 visitors in 2008, with a 3% drop to 753,000 in 2009. This still qualifies as the second highest visitation year for the country. Italy has increased visitation in 5 out of the last 7 years by a total of 347,150 arrivals. Italy accounted for a 1.4% share of 2009 visitor volume.	
9		**South Korea (-2%)**	**744,000**
		Due to a particularly rough first half in 2009, South Korea dropped 2% for the year, despite a strong second-half which saw an average increase in arrivals of more than 12%. South Korea accounted for a 1.4% share of 2009 visitor volume.	
10		Australia (+5%)	724,000
		Australia maintained steady progress and yielded its fifth straight record year with a 5% growth from 2008. Their visitation numbers have nearly doubled over the past 6 years, increasing more than 78%. Australia accounted for a 1.3% share of 2009 visitor volume.	

Top 10 Markets: 2009 International Visitor Spending

Rank		Country	2009 Arrivals
1		**Canada (-13%)**	**$16.2 Billion**
		Canada continued to reside as the top international market for U.S. travel and tourism exports despite a 13% drop in 2009. Their streak of 5 consecutive record-setting years came to an end in 2009 but they still created a $10 billion trade surplus. U.S. travel and tourism exports account for nearly 38% of total U.S. services exports to Canada.	
2		**Japan (-11%)**	**$12.9 Billion**
		Despite an 11% decline in 2009, Japan moved ahead of the U.K. for the 2nd spot on the top-10 list by bringing in close to $13 billion in exports. Japan produced a favorable $8 billion travel and tourism trade balance for the year. U.S. travel and tourism exports account for nearly 31% of total U.S. services exports to Japan.	
3		**United Kingdom (-27%)**	**$12.1 Billion**
		Spending by United Kingdom visitors fell 27% in 2009, after a record-breaking year of $16.7 billion in 2008. This decline was the largest by any country in the top-10, which led to a drop from 2nd to 3rd position. U.S. travel and tourism exports account for nearly 22% of total U.S. services exports to the United Kingdom.	
4		**Mexico (-14%)**	**$8.3 Billion**
		Mexico ended its streak of 5 consecutive record-setting years, by decreasing total spending 14% to $8.3 billion in 2009. Despite the 14% decrease, the trade deficit with Mexico reduced close to $400 million. Mexico's ranking, in terms of international visitor spending, remained unchanged in 2009. U.S. travel and tourism exports account for nearly 38% of total U.S. services exports to Mexico.	
5		**Germany (-16%)**	**$5.6 Billion**
		After a record-breaking 2008 with $6.7 billion spent by international visitors from Germany, the United States saw a 16% drop in spending by its German visitors in 2009. Germany continues to produce the 2nd most total spending dollars out of any country from Europe, behind the United Kingdom. U.S. travel and tourism exports account for nearly 22% of total U.S. services exports to Germany.	

Table (Continued)

Rank		Country	2009 Arrivals
6		**Brazil (+2%)**	**$4.2 Billion**
		Brazil continued to climb up the rankings in 2009, moving from 8th to 6th after being the only country in the top-10 to see an increase in visitor spending. Brazil broke its previous record set in 2008 with its 2% increase in 2009 and now has 6 consecutive years of growth. U.S. travel and tourism exports account for nearly 36% of total U.S. services exports to Brazil.	
7		**France (-12%)**	**$4.2 Billion**
		France moved down a spot in the 2009 rankings due to a 12% decrease in visitor spending coupled with the increased visitation and spending by Brazilians. Even with decreased spending, the trade deficit of $322 million turned around into a surplus of $540 million during the course of 2009. U.S. travel and tourism exports account for nearly 26% of total U.S. services exports to France.	
8		**India (-16%)**	**$3.6 Billion**
		India followed up a record year in 2008 with a loss in visitor spending of 16% in 2009, and dropped a spot in the rankings to #8. India's 16% drop closely resembles the 15% drop the United States saw in total spending from all world visitors combined. U.S. travel and tourism exports account for nearly 36% of total U.S. services exports to India.	
9		**China (-3%)**	**$3.5 Billion**
		Resulting from more pronounced declines from Italy and Australia, China moved into the top-10 ranking for the first time last year, despite a 3% decline in total spending. This 3% reduction comes off the heels of a record year of spending in 2008 of $3.6 billion. U.S. travel and tourism exports account for nearly 23% of total U.S. services to China.	
10		**Australia (-11%)**	**$3.3 Billion**
		In a year when Australia was only 1 of 3 top-10 countries that increased visitation to the United States, their travel and tourism-related spending fell 11% to $3.3 billion. This loss in visitation spending did not have an effect on their standings in the top-10. U.S. travel and tourism exports account for nearly 26% of total U.S. services exports to Australia.	

In: United States Travel and Tourism Industry   ISBN: 978-1-61209-111-2
Editors: D.P. Moore and A.G. Doherty   © 2011 Nova Science Publishers, Inc.

Chapter 5

TESTIMONY OF MARY SAUNDERS, ACTING ASSISTANT SECRETARY FOR MANUFACTURING & SERVICES, INTERNATIONAL TRADE ADMINISTRATION, DEPT. OF COMMERCE, BEFORE THE SENATE COMMERCE, SCIENCE & TRANSPORTATION SUBCOMMITTEE, HEARING ON "TOURISM IN TROUBLED TIMES"[*]

Mary Saunders

INTRODUCTION

Chairman Klobuchar, Ranking Member Martinez, and distinguished members of the committee, thank you for the opportunity to speak with you today concerning the state of the U.S. travel and tourism industry. I welcome your interest in this topic.

---

[*] This is an edited, reformatted and augmented version of remarks delivered as Testimony before the senate commerce, Science and Transportation Subcommittee on Competitiveness, Innovation & Export Promotion dated May 13, 2009

OVERVIEW - STATISTICS

The Department of Commerce's economic accounts data show that the travel and tourism industry generated a record $1.38 trillion in sales for the economy in 2008. The industry directly and indirectly supported more than 8.6 million jobs. From a trade perspective, international travel to the United States represents over one-fourth (26 percent) of all U.S. services exports. In 2008, this translated to $142.1 billion in receipts generated from a record 58 million international visitors. For the 20th consecutive year, travel and tourism produced a travel trade surplus for the United States — a record $29.7 billion — and directly supported more than 900,000 jobs in the United States in 2008.

Canada continues to be the top overall market for international visitors to the United States. Canadian visitors pumped nearly $19 billion into the U.S. economy in 2008, breaking their previous record for the fifth consecutive year. U.S. travel and tourism exports account for 40% of all U.S. services exports to Canada. Spending by Mexican visitors also remained strong for the fifth consecutive year. Travelers from this second top market spent more in the United States on travel and tourism-related goods and services than ever before - $9.8 billion.

Expenditures generated from European visitors also increased substantially in 2008, up 25%. Visitors from the United Kingdom rank second overall in terms of dollars spent on U.S. travel, growing 17% to $17.5 billion. Growth in spending from Germany jumped 26% to $6.5 billion, and growth from France and Italy surged by an incredible 38%, to $4.6 billion and $3.7 billion respectively.

Elsewhere, we saw strong growth in spending by visitors from India and Brazil, increasing by 18% and 26% respectively over 2007 tallies.

Like many other industries, the economic downturn has affected the travel and tourism industry significantly. Although 2008 produced record visitation levels for 13 of the top 25 international markets, visitation showed deepening declines during the fourth quarter of 2008. This trend continued with a 10% drop in visitation levels for the first two months of 2009 compared to the same time last year. This was met by a 13% decline in receipts. The Department's forecast to be released later this month indicates a continued decline for the rest of the year in this valuable export, with a weak recovery expected by the end of 2010.

Most recently, the spread of the H1N1 virus has affected the performance of the industry, compounding the challenges associated with the volatile global economic environment. Department officials met with representatives of nine travel and tourism associations on May 1 to discuss the impact of the situation on the industry. The Secretary's office is receiving weekly status reports from Commerce staff. Industry reports indicate that the impact on travel to the United States and other destinations, with the exception of Mexico, is likely to be minor, provided the flu outbreak continues to subside.

COMMERCE TRAVEL & TOURISM PROMOTION

As these numbers underscore, the travel and tourism industry is important to our nation's economy, employment, and trade. The Department of Commerce works to support the industry through our travel and tourism promotion activities.

As the acting Assistant Secretary for Manufacturing and Services, I oversee the Department of Commerce's Office of Travel and Tourism. My team and I work to remove barriers to the growth of tourism exports and support our Commercial Service offices around the world to assist American travel and tourism businesses and destinations to market and sell their products. We also are the primary government source for travel and tourism statistics.

Within the federal government, we work with the Departments of State and Homeland Security and other federal agencies to develop policies and programs that enhance the competitiveness of the U.S. travel and tourism industry and ensure that we continue to facilitate travel to the United States as we provide for our security. Interagency deliberation on these issues is undertaken through the Tourism Policy Council (TPC), comprising 15 members from federal agencies and offices. We are reinvigorating the Council's role under Secretary Locke's leadership. One of the Council's roles will be to further the coordinating work begun under the now defunct Secure Borders and Open Doors Committee. This Committee had functioned under the Rice-Chertoff Initiative — designed to improve travel procedures for entry to the United States while still meeting security requirements. Commerce Department staff actively served on this Committee which also included private sector representatives. We anticipate the Secretary calling a meeting of the Tourism Policy Council in early Fall.

As you are aware, the Assistant Secretary for Manufacturing & Services also is the Executive Director of the U.S. Travel and Tourism Advisory Board (TTAB), an advisory board consisting of representatives from companies and organizations in the travel and tourism industry appointed by the Secretary.

The Board advises the Secretary on government policies and programs that affect the U.S. travel and tourism industry, offers counsel on current and emerging issues, and provides a forum for discussing and proposing solutions to industry-related problems. We are in the process of organizing a meeting of the Board for later this spring.

Secretary Locke has taken an active interest in the travel and tourism industry. On May 20, he will be in Miami to deliver the keynote luncheon address at International Pow Wow, the top U.S. industry trade show with 5000 buyers and sellers of international travel to the United States. With over 300 foreign and American members of the press in attendance, Pow Wow provides an important opportunity for destinations and businesses to showcase the best that America has to offer for enticing international travelers to our country. The Secretary will be able to relay to all of them the importance of this industry and his gratitude for their dedication and interest in spurring economic recovery and job growth.

CLOSING

The U.S. travel and tourism industry continues to be a key part of our nation's economy. The United States generates more revenue from travel and tourism than any other country in the world. The Department of Commerce has an active program dedicated to expanding travel and tourism business opportunities for employment and economic growth. We look forward to working with the Congress and with the travel and tourism industry on policies and programs that will continue to enhance the competitive position of the United States.

As Secretary Locke said before members of this Committee at his confirmation hearing, "There's a great deal of interest and fascination with America among people all around the world. They think of the great cities of America, but they also think of the great majestic, natural beauty of America from the Grand Canyon to the Badlands and to our incredible, beautiful national parks. And they think of America as a place of great pristine environment, a place to visit, a place for recreation."

I thank the Chairman and the members of the Committee for the opportunity to testify, and I look forward to answering any questions you may have.

In: United States Travel and Tourism Industry   ISBN: 978-1-61209-111-2
Editors: D.P. Moore and A.G. Doherty   © 2011 Nova Science Publishers, Inc.

Chapter 6

TESTIMONY OF JAY S. WITZEL, PRESIDENT AND CEO, CARLSON HOTELS WORLDWIDE, BEFORE THE SENATE COMMERCE, SCIENCE & TRANSPORTATION SUBCOMMITTEE, HEARING ON "THE NATIONAL ECONOMIC IMPACT OF TRAVEL AND TOURISM"[*]

Jay S. Witzel

Chairman Klobuchar, Ranking Member Martinez and other distinguished Members of the Committee: Thank you for the opportunity and privilege to appear before you on behalf of Carlson Hotels Worldwide and the greater Carlson organization. I would particularly like to thank Senator Klobuchar for your leadership in calling this hearing and your passionate support of the travel industry both in our home state of Minnesota and in the national arena.

Carlson is a Minnesota-based company with global hotel, travel, restaurant and marketing businesses that are inter-related in and to the travel industry. I lead Carlson Hotels Worldwide which has over 1,020 hotel locations under five brands. Other parts of Carlson include Carlson Wagonlit

---

[*] This is an edited, reformatted and augmented version Testimony of Jay S. Witzel before Subcommittee on Competitiveness, Innovation & Export Promotion dated May 13, 2009

Travel, T.G.I. Friday's Restaurants and Carlson Marketing which is one of the nation's leading meeting, event and incentive companies. Globally Carlson and its brands employ 160,000 people in more than 150 countries, with over 50,000 of those jobs here in the United States. The jobs of these individuals and the overall vibrancy of our businesses are reliant on the health of the travel industry.

Specifically today, I would like to address the topic of business related travel, including travel for meetings, conferences, events and performance incentives. Business travel creates 2.4 million American jobs, $240 billion in spending and $39 billion in tax revenues. These statistics are provided by the U.S. Travel Association of which Carlson is a member.

This part of our industry has been the source of undeserved and crippling attacks in recent months. Critics have mislabeled many meetings and events as unnecessary and frivolous, causing companies that have received federal government support---plus many more that have not---to cancel business travel activities. An environment has been created in America where legitimate business travel is being questioned and cancelled. This translates into additional loss of jobs, taxes and travel-related revenues for an industry that is already hard- hit from the general economic recession.

Business travel is not an optional luxury or a perk of well-paid executives. Meetings mean business in the American economy. There is no substitute for the face-to-face, hand-to-hand and heart-to-heart results of business meetings. They are a strategic tool for training, education, sales, customer interface, new product development and motivating performance. All of these are vital in rebuilding America's economy and creating new jobs that we so badly need at this time.

But the trend is ominous. According to estimates by Smith Travel Research and the U.S. Travel Association, meetings, events and incentive cancellations in January and February of 2009 resulted in more than $1.9 billion in lost travel spending and cost nearly 20,000 America jobs. Nearly 200,000 travel-related jobs were lost in 2008 and an additional 247,000 will be cut this year, according to data compiled by the U.S. Department of Labor. Those who are losing their jobs represent the hard working faces of America: bellmen, room attendants, banquet servers and cooks.

With so much at stake, we seek your support on three key fronts. First, we are asking all members of Congress and federal policy makers to change the rhetoric that labels business travel, meetings and incentive travel as frivolous and unnecessary. The unintended consequence of this mischaracterization is job loss, lost tax revenues and further stress on this important industry.

Second, we ask your support for a unified set of meeting standards for companies receiving emergency government assistance funds that have been developed by the hotel, travel, meeting and incentive industries. These guidelines have been submitted to the Treasury Department as a policy for these companies to guide them in organizing justifiable meetings, events and incentive travel. They also represent a common sense approach that would apply to any business. They serve as a standard of "best practices" for corporations to conduct meetings, incentives and events with complete transparency and accountability.

And finally, you will also be hearing this morning about another vital initiative to build the vibrancy of America's travel industry: The Travel Promotion Act. We fully support this pending legislation as a foundational strategy to create jobs in travel, tourism and hospitality. It will make America more competitive in the global travel market and grow the nation's inbound travel.

Americans who are part of the travel industry, "getting America moving again" literally is the solution. Today, we ask for your support in making that happen.

Thank you again Chairman Kiobuchar, Ranking Member Martinez and other Members of the Committee for your leadership and engagement on these issues.

In: United States Travel and Tourism Industry   ISBN: 978-1-61209-111-2
Editors: D.P. Moore and A.G. Doherty   © 2011 Nova Science Publishers, Inc.

Chapter 7

TESTIMONY OF SAM GILLILAND, CHAIRMAN AND CEO, SABRE HOLDINGS CORPORATION, BEFORE THE SENATE COMMERCE, SCIENCE & TRANSPORTATION SUBCOMMITTEE, HEARING ON "TOURISM IN TROUBLED TIMES"*

Sam Gilliland

Chairwoman Klobuchar, Senator Martinez, Members of the Committee, my name is Sam Gilliland, and I am Chairman and CEO of Sabre Holdings, the world's largest travel distribution company. Among our businesses are the Sabre global distribution system, which powers corporate and leisure travel agencies, and Travelocity.com, the online travel company that gives consumers the opportunity at any time, day or night, to find and compare amazing travel bargains in the U.S. and around the world. Today, I'll share with you a sampling of these deals that I hope will push Americans out of their nests and back into the air to destinations both here and abroad.

---

* This is an edited, reformatted and augmented version of Testimony by Sam Gilliland before United States Senate Subcommittee on Competitiveness, Innovation & Export Promotion dated May 13, 2009

TRAVEL IS GOOD

At Sabre, we firmly believe that "Travel is Good." Let me tell you what the button I'm wearing means. Travel is good for the economy and for business, it's good for our nation's jobs, it's good for our states and our local communities, it's good for connecting us with our families and friends, and it's good for understanding and enjoying the many diverse cultures and peoples of the world. Travel is good for America, Madam Chairwoman. But the state of the travel industry in America today is not good. I hope we can leave this hearing today dedicated to making it better together.

For every dollar spent on travel, the US Travel Association (of which Sabre is a member) estimates that $2.34 of additional spending cascades through the economy. With that sort of multiplier for a sector that represents $740 billion in spending each year, travel and tourism can provide not just a stimulus, but a jolt, to the U.S. economy if Congress and the Administration were to put policies in place that help, rather than hinder, its recovery.

I've attached to my testimony a listing of some of the most compelling offers available in 2009 – what we're calling "The Year of the Travel Deal." When you and your constituents are ready to take that vacation, to a theme park, National Park or beach via cruise, air or car, Travelocity has some of the best values on the planet at prices straight from the 1960's. They include:

- Orlando theme parks from $34 a night with free admission for kids.
- Alaska cruises for $47 a night.
- Hotels near Glacier National Park in Montana at 35% off.
- Puerto Rico discounts combining $200 off air+hotel packages and a night free for every three paid nights.
- $400 discounts on Bermuda hotels and packages.

All of these deals, and many more, are offered on Travelocity.com, along with their applicable terms and conditions. That's the good news.

But here's the bad: The remarkable online consumer deals and prices found in the marketplace today must be put in context. They are not likely to be around for long. Eventually, just as airlines have opted to park airplanes in the desert rather than operate them at a loss, hotels and resorts and cruise lines will eventually reduce their inventory of properties and ships if they cannot realize an acceptable return on these assets; and in fact we're already starting to see that occur. Put another way, for our industry to regain its footing and stimulate the economy as we know it can, it first has to achieve economic sustainability. That's a term that resonates for me, as I serve as the Chairman of the Economic Sustainability Subcommittee of the U.S. Travel and Tourism Advisory Board, a group of travel industry executives appointed by the Secretary of Commerce to provide him with policy guidance. Our group will tell Secretary Locke in its final report that there is much work to be done to achieve economic sustainability in the travel and tourism sector. That's also the message I'd like to deliver to you today.

Here are some of the sobering year on year booking trends we are seeing in the travel and tourism industry:

- The volume of domestic air travel and hotel stays made by corporations are both down nearly 20 percent, with airfares and price of hotel stays down seven percent.
- The volume of domestic air travel for leisure is down almost five percent and average airfares are down 10 percent.

Behind these numbers are legions of people -- your constituents and our industry's employees -- whose jobs have either been eliminated or are at risk. At one independent Chicago hotel, the front desk staff was recently cut in half and the reservation and revenue teams were eliminated with the exception of one director. Nearby, a midsize chain hotel conducted major layoffs, and for those employees who remain, the hotel has eliminated 401 K matching and imposed salary cuts. This is typical of what is happening around the country.

Also travelers, whose rear-ends are not in airplane seats and whose heads are not in hotel beds, are not bringing their tourism dollars to spend on dinners, taxis, theater tickets, tips and more. Taken together, these statistics, which feature many double digit declines in volume and price, paint a picture of an industry with unsustainable economics that is contributing far less than it could to the recovery of the U.S. economy.

Our country and the world are on sale because the travel and tourism industry is reeling from a perfect storm of crisis, fear and ignorance. In recent months, we've experienced the worst economic downturn in 80 years; a swine flu outbreak that is serious and demands precaution, but has spawned an "infodemic" that has led to unhelpful panic; unstable fuel prices that were a major factor in leading airlines to park aircraft that would otherwise be productively flying people to meetings and conventions in Las Vegas and Orlando; corporations that are fearful they will be publicly criticized for holding legitimate meetings and conventions, which are proven and effective business tools; and a crumbling U.S. aviation infrastructure that, as Chairman Rockefeller memorably reminded us, currently ranks behind Mongolia's.

This does not have to be so. From a policy perspective, there are several key and often inter-related initiatives that will help us out of our malaise and, therefore, require your urgent attention. They include energy policy, air traffic control modernization, environmental policy, and Treasury travel guidelines.

ENERGY POLICY

We must reduce American dependence on foreign oil and provide incentives for alternative energy research and deployment. Today, there simply is insufficient competition to petroleum-based fuels -- oil has travel and tourism "over a barrel." We're seeing encouraging work in developing alternatives to jet fuel for aircraft engines as well as alternatives to gasoline for automobiles, but more needs to be done to expedite this work for the sake of our nation's security and prosperity.

The International Air Transport Association (IATA) has established a 10 percent target for alternative jet fuels by 2017. Recent tests by Continental Airlines, JAL Airlines, Air New Zealand and Virgin Atlantic Airlines prove that next generation sustainable biofuels (such as algae, camelina and jatropha) work, and there is even a possibility for improved fuel efficiency. Certification for some of these fuels by 2010 or 2011 is a real possibility, but much more work needs to be done to bring these fuels into commercial production.

Currently, there are many viable alternatives to gasoline to power automobiles, including ethanol, methanol, plug in hybrids and more. We need to require car- makers to equip more vehicles with flexible fuel converters, which will create an incentive for those who would bring alternative fuels to market.

Our objective isn't necessarily to eliminate oil as a transportation fuel, but to provide incentives for viable competition to it. The potential benefits of alternative fuels are enormous, including up to an 80 percent reduction in emissions over the fuel's life-cycle and increased energy security for our nation. A biofuel industry could also be a major generator of employment and wealth for the U.S. and the developing world, and that's why I'm supportive of your efforts, Chairwoman Klobuchar, in S. 835 to drive open fuel standards for automobile manufacturers.

The nation's airlines and airports, in a very real sense, are the key parts of a transportation grid that is every bit as vital as the power grid to our national economy. When you get right down to it, energy and travel and tourism are closely intertwined. Without access to sustainable – by which I mean predictable, abundant, affordable and environmentally sound – energy to move business and leisure travelers as well as goods to their destinations, our industry could not exist. And this applies not only to airplanes, but also to cars, buses, trucks, ships and trains.

Last summer, oil prices skyrocketed, reaching a peak of $147 per barrel in July 2008 and were the subject of much debate in the Senate. These soaring oil prices threatened the U.S. economy, and our nation's airlines and airports were in an especially precarious position. Fuel jumped ahead of labor and equipment costs to become the number one airline expense. Data showed that if these soaring costs did not abate, we would soon see major U.S. airlines fail and many more U.S. airports close, and in so doing, threaten our primary means of intercity transportation, millions of jobs and our American way of life. To stay alive, airlines began cutting capacity in September 2008 to levels that were last seen in 2002 when they were trying to recover from 9/11.

Since then, the price of oil has fallen dramatically – at one point to the mid $30s per barrel, and currently hovering just below $60 per barrel. However, while the acute crisis of massive energy-related failures has temporarily abated (largely because the worldwide demand for oil has dropped dramatically in step with the global financial crisis and recession), the chronic problem of wildly fluctuating oil prices remains unsolved, and in time will once again devastate travel and tourism – and jeopardize our national security and broader economic well-being – unless we demand and secure a sound energy policy from the current Administration and Congress.

I'm encouraged that energy policy is one of President Obama's announced policy priorities, and significant funding for R&D tax incentives for alternative fuel figures prominently in his proposed budget. I support these initiatives; they must remain a priority. We must insist on a comprehensive U.S. energy policy that will, among many other benefits, deliver travel and tourism from its current unacceptable and unsustainable situation.

AIR TRAFFIC CONTROL MODERNIZATION

Lost in the debate about funding the long-overdue "NextGen" Air Traffic Control (ATC) systems, is the astonishing and sad fact that the navigation systems used in cars and mobile phones today are light years ahead of the technology used in our nation's ATC systems. Modernization of the U.S. air transportation network cannot wait any longer – it is a bankable way to achieve much needed energy, environmental and customer-service improvements for our nation's aviation industry. "NextGen" must become "NowGen." I am pleased that the Senate's Aviation Operations, Safety and Security Subcommittee is holding a hearing on

FAA Reauthorization later this afternoon, in which perspectives on industry participants will be heard. I expect "NowGen" will be a focus.

We can no longer afford inaction. Even with lower traffic volumes, U.S. air space continues to be overcrowded in many places, causing costly flight delays and forcing airlines to operate inefficiently. This adds unnecessary expense for both airlines and the travelling public. Despite significant advances in available modern-day technology, our airlines are forced to find their way using ground- based navigation points, a method that is only a few small steps ahead of where we were in the early days of aviation, when railways and bon fires were used for air navigation. The radar system used today to guide U.S. flights is more than 40 years old, which may help explain why nearly one-quarter of all those flights are late. If we do it right, ATC modernization will:

- Allow all airplanes to fly more direct, efficient routes, significantly reducing fuel burn and CO_2 emissions,
- Reduce congestion and open up access – more flights – in crowded airspace,
- Reduce flight delays and inconvenience to passengers and shippers,
- Create or save 77,000 jobs, and
- Be transformational for the broader economy.

"NowGen" MUST become a national priority, not only in words, but in action. There are enormous benefits that flow from timely action, including an improved transportation infrastructure and economic stimulus as well as positive impacts on the environment and, of course, on travelers. It will also encourage, rather than impede, sustainable growth in the airline industry.

In these troubled times for the tourism industry, all industry participants should be committed to working with Congress, the Administration and, most importantly, each other to ensure ATC modernization will be done early, right and in a way that transforms air travel in this country and keeps the U.S. competitive on the world stage.

ENVIRONMENTAL POLICY

We must establish policies to reduce greenhouse gasses that threaten our environment, and insist that the burdens of such policies take into account the international dimensions of the problem, and be fairly shared so they don't fall disproportionately on the travel and tourism industry.

In particular, we must not unfairly scapegoat the airline industry, which has done much to make itself more energy efficient as a matter of economic necessity. U.S. airlines have a longstanding commitment to improving fuel efficiency and, therefore, reducing their carbon footprint. Since 1978, the Air Transport Association reports that its member airlines have improved fuel efficiency by 110 percent, which has resulted in significant reductions of CO_2 emissions. The airlines' impact on the environment is relatively small: airlines today account for between two and three percent of the world's man-made carbon emissions.

As legislation concerning carbon emissions is considered, it's important to simultaneously pursue global approaches to aviation emissions to ensure fairness and equity to all participants. If revenue related to carbon emissions is raised from the commercial aviation industry, it should be re-directed back into aviation-related environmental and efficiency improvements. Further financial burdens on our economically challenged industry must be weighed with extreme care to avoid negative impacts, not only to the airlines, but also to the cities and communities they serve and the jobs they generate.

TREASURY TRAVEL GUIDELINES

Paralyzing confusion abounds in our industry, and in corporations, about what the Treasury Department considers "luxury" and "excessive" expenditures in the area of business travel. Meetings, conventions and incentive travel are proven business tools that allow companies to establish valuable relationships, solicit feedback and reward employees. Of course, these tools must be used responsibly by all corporations. Unfortunately, given the state of uncertainty, many companies are opting not to engage in any form of business travel, even when that means forfeiting large deposits and foregoing important business opportunities. This makes no sense at all. Many of these companies are customers of our company, and because we provide travel policy automation solutions to them, many have asked us for guidance.

Sabre's GetThere division is in the process of developing a formal education and consulting solution for corporations, which will focus on managing corporate governance and compliance, reducing unnecessary travel and driving accountability. We intend to be part of the solution that will help all companies make wise travel decisions. However, the Treasury Department needs to do its part in giving clear, specific guidance to our industry. I understand that Treasury is expected to weigh in soon in this area, but it is not clear how detailed and satisfactory this guidance will be.

I urge this Committee to watch these developments carefully and encourage Treasury to stem the continuing confusion in the marketplace about which travel policies are acceptable and which are not. Travel and tourism cannot absorb further paralysis and retrenchment based on fear of criticism and negative publicity. Treasury should provide a framework, and with it peace of mind, so all businesses can confidently conduct legitimate meetings, events and incentive travel.

The US Travel Association has developed such a framework that has been widely supported by our industry. A timely endorsement of these model guidelines by the Treasury Department would provide businesses with the peace of mind they require.

CONCLUSION

Our troubled industry has a number of pressing problems that demand urgent action in Washington. Energy, infrastructure and environmental reforms should be included at the top of the priority list. These issues are intertwined and therefore making a positive difference on one will lead to positive differences on the others. Glenn Tilton, CEO of United Airlines, put it best when he said that these reforms create and complete a "virtuous circle." Moving forward with ATC modernization reduces demand for fuel and, thus, the carbon footprint of our industry. If we can move forward on finding solutions to these problems, we will take a giant leap toward economic sustainability.

We must also give corporations the confidence that they can once again hold business meetings and conventions in order to achieve their corporate objectives. Timely guidance from the Treasury Department, in the form of an endorsement of the US Travel Association's model guidelines is urgently needed.

The storm clouds that have been hanging over our industry do have a silver lining. They provide an unprecedented opportunity for our industry's participants – airlines, hotels and resorts, car rental companies, cruise lines, technology providers, travel agents, tour operators, convention and visitor bureaus (CVBs), union groups and corporate and leisure travelers – to come together to look for ways we can cooperate and make a difference on major policy issues that impact not just some of us, but all of us. As the largest industry in the world, we are an inherently powerful, but historically fragmented, industry. But I believe we are realizing that we can have an impact that befits our importance when we work more closely together and with policymakers who understand our role and want to help us succeed.

It is an honor to be invited here today to speak to you about tourism in troubled times, although I am looking forward to the day when I can come back and speak about tourism in stable, if not booming, times. I hope this hearing proves to be one of the watershed events that helps put our industry back on the flight path toward a better future. Chairwoman Klobuchar, I commend you for taking the time to hear from our industry. Your interest is strong validation that travel and tourism is vital to our country and its prosperity.

The impact that Congress and the Administration can have on the health of travel and tourism is profound, not just in the legislation you pass, but also in the signals you send, particularly now. Words do matter, especially when they come from our leaders in Washington. As you speak about this industry and consider policy matters that impact our recovery and well-being, I encourage you to act deliberately and remember that "Travel is Good" for America. Thank you again for the opportunity to testify today.

In: United States Travel and Tourism Industry   ISBN: 978-1-61209-111-2
Editors: D.P. Moore and A.G. Doherty   © 2011 Nova Science Publishers, Inc.

Chapter 8

TESTIMONY OF JAY RASULO, CHAIRMAN, WALT DISNEY PARKS AND RESORTS, BEFORE THE SENATE COMMERCE, SCIENCE & TRANSPORTATION SUBCOMMITTEE, HEARING ON "TOURISM IN TROUBLED TIMES"[*]

Jay Rasulo

I appreciate the opportunity to be here today to discuss America's competitive position in travel and tourism—and to explain how increasing foreign travel to the United States can play a vital role in our nation's economic recovery.

I come wearing two hats, both as immediate past Chairman of the U.S. Travel Association--which represents a $740 billion industry employing 7.7 million Americans--and as Chairman of Walt Disney Parks and Resorts, which employs 90,000 people and operates 11 theme parks on three continents, a top-rated cruise line, a major tour wholesaler and more than 34,000 hotel rooms.

---

[*] This is an edited, reformatted and augmented version of Testimony of Jay Rasulo before the Senate Subcommittee on Competitiveness, Innovation & Export Promotion of United States Senate Committee on Commerce, Science and Transportation dated May 13, 2009

The travel industry is vital to our nation's economic health. It generates $2 billion in spending every *day*, and provides $115 billion in tax revenue to the federal, state and local governments. But along with the rest of the economy, the travel industry has suffered during this recession, incurring its share of lost revenue and jobs.

Ladies and gentlemen, there is a way we can stem these losses, improve the nation's competitive edge and advance America's public diplomacy--by forging a partnership between government and industry to promote international travel to the U.S. And the time to act is now.

Two years ago, I had the honor of testifying before you to present a document called "A Blueprint to Discover America," which looked at how we can regain our nation's once-dominant position in the market for international travel. After 9/11, overseas travel to the U.S. dropped significantly and has never fully recovered. Competition from foreign travel destinations increased significantly, and that is something we can't change. In addition many overseas visitors stopped coming to America because they perceived they were no longer welcome here. That is something we can change.

Back in 2007, we had the luxury of talking about the —Blueprint‖ as a way to *gain* jobs and revenue. But now, in the midst of recession, it's painfully clear how much we've *lost* by not fully implementing the Blueprint. Overseas visitors spend an estimated $4,500 per person when they come here, and if arrivals had kept pace with global trends since 2001, that would have totaled $182 *billion* in spending. That's enough to support 245,000 jobs. Moreover, the added revenue generated by those visits would have yielded $27 billion in tax receipts.

The "Blueprint to Discover America" recommended improvements in three areas critical to attracting new international visitors. And thanks to the efforts of Congress, we have had some important achievements. But much more work remains.

First, we need a secure, but user-friendly, visa process. We applaud Congress for expanding the Visa Waiver program, but for those travelers requiring a visa, the system needs to be more efficient and easier to navigate— while continuing to put America's security first.

Second, we need to continue making the entry process a more positive experience—something that is already starting to happen thanks to the Model Ports program to improve our nation's busiest airports.

Third, we need to promote the United States abroad—and that is where the most work remains. We need to tell the world about the improvements we have made to the entry process. We need to invite international travelers to visit the United States. We need to tell them that they are welcome here.

The Travel Promotion Act– introduced yesterday by Senators Dorgan and Ensign, and co-sponsored by Chairman Klobuchar and Ranking Member Martinez, among others – would create a public-private entity that could speak with the authority of the United States government to tell the world, "We want you to visit." It would work to reverse widespread negative perceptions that the U.S. is unwelcoming to overseas travelers. And it would complement and augment our nation's public diplomacy efforts: We know from research that those who have visited the U.S. are 74% more likely to have an extremely favorable opinion of America than those who haven't traveled here.

This new entity would combine the expertise of the private sector with the oversight and coordination of the federal government. It would serve as the primary voice for all travel-related policies. It would coordinate our national strategies to maximize the benefits of travel to America. And it would ensure that international travel benefits *all* 50 states and the District of Columbia, including areas not traditionally visited by foreigners.

We are only asking the United States to establish what nearly every other major foreign market already has: a nationally coordinated and well-funded travel promotion campaign. To give you an idea of just how competitive the overseas travel market has become: Greece and Mexico each spend $150 million a year on promotion campaigns to attract travelers; China spends $60 million; France, Germany, Italy and the U.K. spend a combined $250 million.

It is important to point out that in these times when the Congress is understandably wary of new spending, the Travel Promotion Act would use NO taxpayer dollars. Instead, it would be funded through a small fee collected from overseas visitors, combined with matching funds from the travel industry. This isn't a free ride for industry. We will be contributing our fair share to make it work.

Indeed, we are already contributing. Recently, Walt Disney Parks and Resorts funded and produced a $2.5 million video to welcome overseas travelers to the United States, which we donated to the U.S. government. You can now see that video at several of the nation's busiest airports, at 105 American consulate and embassy offices around the world, and even on some airlines just before arriving in the U.S. And, thanks to the interest of this Subcommittee, you will see it here today.

The idea behind the video was that if you make the entry process a more welcoming experience, more international travelers will visit our shores.

The starting point for this project was to decide what story to tell (creating compelling stories, after all, is what Disney does best). As we considered the options, we realized that America's greatest story is her people...their friendliness, their openness, their hospitality. That's what visitors find most remarkable when they come to the United States. And that is why we chose to showcase the people of America in this Welcome Video.

From the time visitors apply for a visa in a consulate overseas, to their arrival at an airport here in the States, they will be greeted by the ordinary people who make this nation extraordinary. And through every step of the entry process, the message to these visitors will be expressed in a single word, with universal meaning.

Welcome.

I thank you again for the opportunity to speak here today, and I look forward to addressing your questions.

May we please show the video.

In: United States Travel and Tourism Industry   ISBN: 978-1-61209-111-2
Editors: D.P. Moore and A.G. Doherty   © 2011 Nova Science Publishers, Inc.

Chapter 9

TESTIMONY OF ROSSI RALENKOTTER, PRESIDENT AND CEO, LAS VEGAS CONVENTION AND VISITORS AUTHORITY, LAS VEGAS, NEVADA, BEFORE THE SENATE COMMERCE, SCIENCE & TRANSPORTATION SUBCOMMITTEE, HEARING ON "TOURISM IN TROUBLED TIMES"*

Rossi Ralenkotter

Good morning Senators and thank you for the invitation to participate in today's hearing. As you are aware, May 9-17 is National Travel and Tourism Week. Yesterday in Las Vegas, hundreds of individuals rallied at the Las Vegas Convention Center in a show of unity and pride for what travel and tourism provides to Southern Nevada. It is the number one industry for Las Vegas. In fact, the travel and tourism industry is the number one economic stimulus for the entire State of Nevada.

---

* This is an edited, reformatted and augmented version of Testimony of Rossi Ralenkotter before the Senate Committee on Commerce, Science and Transportation dated May 13, 2009

Approximately 250,000 people in Las Vegas are employed because of tourism. Three of every 10 jobs in Las Vegas are directly related to travel and tourism. The industry generates more than $30 billion for the local economy ever year. Over the past 50 years, room tax revenue generated by leisure tourists and conventions and meetings delegates has contributed approximately $2 billion to help fund the construction of schools, roads, parks and other local government services.

Over the last two decades, Las Vegas has evolved into more than a gaming destination. We offer world-class entertainment, exquisite dining and fabulous shopping, in addition to the finest resorts anywhere in the world. Las Vegas has over 140,000 hotel rooms, more than any other destination and we are scheduled to add an additional 13,000 rooms to our inventory this year. Hotel occupancy is traditionally 25 percent points higher than the national average.

Las Vegas hosts approximately 38 million visitors annually. Eight-five percent of our visitors are leisure travelers, and 15 percent are business travelers. Las Vegas hosts more than 22,000 meetings, conventions and trade shows every year. Fortune 500 companies routinely meet in Las Vegas and conduct business. For 15 consecutive years, Las Vegas has been the number one trade show destination in North America, according to the *Tradeshow Week 200*, a trade media publication that analyzes data from all destinations. In fact, this week we have RECON – the Global Retail Real Estate Convention – formerly known as the International Council of Shopping Centers Show – in Las Vegas.

As we analyze the current trends and data for Las Vegas, I can absolutely say the current recession has had the most severe impact on the industry than ever before. I refer to it as the "imperfect storm" because there are so many variables that have contributed to the downturn: gas prices, housing foreclosures, the banking system collapse, volatility in the stock market, airline cutbacks, unemployment and challenges for the meetings and conventions market. We began to see a softening of the Las

Vegas market around the middle of last year and all indicators began to drop dramatically when fall arrived. For 2008, visitation was down 4.4 percent, attendance at meetings and conventions decreased 5 percent and the number of airline passengers coming into and leaving McCarran International Airport was down almost 8 percent.

Through the first three months of 2009, visitor volume is down almost 9 percent, passenger traffic and McCarran is off 14 percent, and convention attendance is down 29 percent, a reflection of the economy but also because of the regular industry practice of some shows rotating cities for their event.

Unemployment is at its highest rate in more than 25 years and is at 10.4 percent. Approximately 16-thousand people in the travel and tourism industry in the State of Nevada have lost their job within the last year because of the recession.

Las Vegas is a microcosm of the entire tourism industry. And while many of the challenges are because of the recession, there are long-term issues we also must address. Foremost, is the tremendous disadvantage the travel and tourism industry faces when competing with other countries. Travel and tourism is one of America's most successful industries, generating a trade surplus that helps offset the nation's trade deficit. While international travel has boomed over the past several years, with 49 million more overseas trips booked in 2008 than in 2000, America actually lost visitors, welcoming 633,000 fewer overseas travelers last year. If the Unites States had simply kept pace with the growth in global overseas travel, 58 million more overseas travelers would have visited the United States in that period and 245,000 new jobs would be been created in 2008 alone.

Every developed nation – except for the United States – operates a nationally coordinated travel promotion campaign. Other countries outspend the United States by enormous amounts when promoting travel and tourism. According to the World Travel Organization, Greece spends more than $151 million to promote the travel industry. Spain sends nearly $120 million, Australia over $1 13 million and the United Kingdom more than $89 million. Canada spends $58 million and that will probably increase with the 2010 Winter Olympics in Vancouver. The United States spends approximately $6 million.

The Travel Promotion Act would address this issue and help create new jobs. It would provide a national platform – brand U.S.A. – for the country and states could leverage the brand with their own marketing efforts. It would be similar to what Las Vegas has done. The Las Vegas Convention and Visitors Authority provides the brand marketing platform for the destination, and private industry resorts develop marketing campaigns to attract visitors to their specific properties and attractions. The Travel Promotion Act will help address the tremendous disadvantage the United States has when competing for travelers with other countries. We appreciate the leadership of Senator Byron Dorgan and Nevada's own Senator John Ensign, Majority Leader Harry Reid and the United States Travel Association on this proposed legislation.

The other long-term issue we need to address is the mindset or perception of some that business travel is not a worthwhile investment. On the contrary, it is a necessary investment. The National Association of Broadcasters holds its annual trade show in Las Vegas and the organization reported that more than $68 billion of business was secured from the 2008 event because of the face-to-face meetings on the trade show floor. The industry trade organization Meetings Professional International released a study this spring that showed face-to-face meetings is still the most valuable sales tool for organizations. Even with all the technology today, a face-to-face meeting is still required to lay the foundation or finalize a business agreement.

Recently, the meetings and convention industry has received a lot of attention, especially the incentive-based travel programs. It caused many corporations – both those receiving TARP funds – and those who did not receive TARP funds – to postpone, reschedule or cancel their business travel. In Las Vegas, the impact was 402 cancelled meetings and more than $166 million in lost business. This directly impacted the 46,000 individuals who work in this particular industry segment in Las Vegas. We certainly understand the need for accountability for those companies receiving TARP funds. However, the concept of federal meetings guidelines for those organizations receiving federal aid may be a solution to address accountability while not harming an industry that contributes nearly $16 billion in tax revenue to federal, state and local levels. When the meetings and convention industry is harmed, individual jobs, small businesses, corporations and the national economy are impacted.

In these trying economic times, we are all looking for ways to stimulate the economy. The Travel and Tourism Industry is one of the answers. We need to encourage people to travel for leisure and to attend trade shows and meetings – both domestically and internationally. Travel and tourism is the number one, two or three economic stimulus in most states. For Las Vegas, and Nevada, it is the number one industry. Long-term, the future of Las Vegas is bright and our brand is strong.

In: United States Travel and Tourism Industry   ISBN: 978-1-61209-111-2
Editors: D.P. Moore and A.G. Doherty   © 2011 Nova Science Publishers, Inc.

Chapter 10

RESTORING AMERICA'S TRAVEL BRAND: NATIONAL STRATEGY TO COMPETE FOR INTERNATIONAL VISITORS[*]

U.S. Travel and Tourism Advisory Board

I. ENVIRONMENTAL ASSESSMENT

Introduction: A New Golden Age of World Travel

It is safe to say that the world is now entering a new golden age for travel and tourism. A confluence of developments is fueling an era of explosive growth in the world travel market – which is likely to drive a sizable share of the world's future job creation, economic growth and tax revenue. Simply put, travel and tourism, which includes leisure, business, conventions and meetings, educational and medical travel, is one of – if not the most – significant growth industries in the world today.

First, rising disposable income means that vast new markets are joining the world travel community. The market is growing by tens of

---

[*] This is an edited, reformatted and augmented of Restoring America's Travel Brand   National Strategy to Compete for Inernational Visitors, dated September 5, 2006.

millions of individuals each year. The number of country-to-country travelers is projected to double within 15 years,[1] and the revenue generated by this business and leisure travel is projected to double within 10 years.[2]

Second, the number of world class travel destinations is proliferating, due to improvements in travel infrastructure and facilities, as well as the easing of restrictions in many parts of the world that were previously inaccessible.

Third, the new technology and Internet and mobile communication devices allows for enhanced access to information, greater mobility, and shared cultural experiences on a scale never seen before. Individuals, as well as travel agents, meeting planners and other intermediaries in all corners of the planet are increasingly aware of the expanding array of travel options, and the competition for their business is growing both more intense and more sophisticated.

Countries that adapt to these new realities will position themselves to reap a windfall of new jobs and economic growth. Those countries that do not, will risk being left behind.

Within this fast-growing market, consumer expectations, behaviors and booking patterns are also evolving at breakneck speed. Today's world travelers not only originate from more countries, but also more money to spend, an increasing number of worthwhile destinations to choose from, better access to information, and they expect a higher level of service and ease of movement than ever before. In short, they expect nations to *compete* for their business.

In this paper, the U.S. Travel and Tourism Advisory Board[3] examines the competitive position of the U.S. within the world travel and tourism industry, and recommends a new national strategy to compete for a greater share of this growing market.

The State of American Competitiveness

Looking solely at the number of – and revenue generated by – visitors to the United States, it is easy to conclude that the U.S. position remains strong. Arrivals to the U.S. – including both trans-border and long-haul travel – are on an upward track, and this year may surpass the record previously set in 2000. This view is also supported by the fact that the U.S. generates far more revenue from international arrivals than any other country in the world.

But a closer analysis reveals troubling indicators that suggest the U.S. competitive position is not nearly as strong as it should be.

At a time when other countries have become better funded, more coordinated and sophisticated in their efforts to attract international visitors, the U.S. still lacks a national strategy to compete. This situation puts the U.S. at a distinct competitive disadvantage in efforts to attract world travel.

The U.S. still lacks a national strategy to compete for world travel

The consequences of this competitive gap have already materialized. A close analysis of key indicators and trend lines reveals that beneath the surface of seemingly good news, the U.S. has been steadily losing market share for years, at a cost of hundreds of billions of dollars and millions of jobs.

Number of Visitors	
The Good:	**The Bad:**
In 2006, the U.S. is projected to return to – and possibly surpass – the levels of international arrivals last reached in 2000.	The U.S. has captured 0% of the nearly 20% growth in country-to-country travel since 2000.[4] By the end of 2005, North America was the *only sub-region of the world to have recorded a decline in arrivals since 2000.*[5]

Market Share	
The Good:	**The Bad:**
The U.S. captured 6.1% of the 808 million international travelers in 2005 – ranking third behind France and Spain.[6] This represents a second year increase in market share.	U.S. share of international travel has fallen 35% since 1992 – from a high of 9.4% to the current 6.1%. Had the U.S. maintained its share of the world travel market, 27 million more travelers would have visited the U.S. in 2005.[8]
The U.S. captured 12% of the $622 billion in revenue that was spent by country-to-country travelers in 2004 – by far the highest ranking among countries in the world.[7]	U.S. share of revenue from international travel has fallen 29% since 1992 – costing the U.S. an estimated $43 billion in 2005 alone. The cumulative cost since 1992 is estimated at $286 billion in economic growth and millions of jobs.[9] For the cumulative effect on U.S. GDP growth, see the chart below:

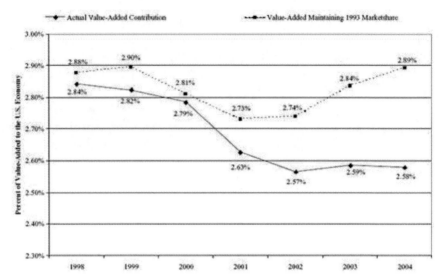

Source: U.S. Department of Commerce Bureau of Economic Analysis

Loss of U.S. Marketshare: Effect on GDP Growth

Revenue	
The Good:	**The Bad:**
The U.S. leads the world in international travel and tourism receipts. The U.S. gained 65% more revenue from international visitors than Spain and 83% more revenue than France.[10]	In 2004 – the most recent year for which world statistics are available – the U.S. took in $8 billion less from foreign visitors than it did in 2000, at the same time that total world receipts were $149 billion higher.[11]
	Meanwhile, lucrative overseas travel to the U.S. is still down 16.5% from 2000, with corresponding revenues down 8% in 2005.[12]

Balance of Trade	
The Good:	**The Bad:**
The travel and tourism trade surplus rose to $7.4 billion in 2005, an increase of 84% over 2004 and the second year in a row the surplus has nearly doubled.	Compared to 10 years ago, the U.S. international tourism balance of trade has *declined nearly 72% – from $26.3 billion in* 1996 to $7.4 billion in 2005.[13]

Brand Strength	
The Good:	**The Bad:**
The U.S. benefits from perhaps the widest, richest array of tourism attractions in the world, as well as a world class level of service, infrastructure and hospitality facilities.	The U.S. has fallen from 1st to 6th among dream destinations for international travelers.[14] An international survey of professional travel agents and purchasers showed that 77 percent believed that the U.S. is more difficult to visit than other destinations, while only six percent found it easier.[15]

The Need for a National Strategy

Promoting travel to the United States is in the national interest – in terms of jobs, economic growth and national reputation.

Economic Rewards. Every one percent of world market share that the U.S. regains will result in an estimated 8.1 million more visitors; $13.4 billion in additional revenues; 153,000 additional U.S. jobs; $3.5 billion in additional payroll; and $2 billion in additional tax revenues.[16]

Diplomatic Rewards. The State Department spends more than $800 million on programs designed to communicate America's values to other countries and cultures, through exchange, information programs and other public relations activities.[17]

Promoting travel to the United States is in the national interest – in terms of jobs, economic growth and national reputation

For a fraction of this cost, the travel and tourism industry can be a powerful partner in these efforts. The simple act of ASKING people to visit us – whether through marketing or friendlier borders – will demonstrate to the world that we are an open, welcoming and friendly society.

For these reasons, the U.S. Travel and Tourism Advisory Board offers the following recommendations for a national strategy to gain competitive advantage in the world travel and tourism market.

The Elements of a National Strategy

1. **Make it easier for people to visit, by balancing hospitality with security.** A June 2006 survey of international travel agents and purchasers showed that 77% believe the United States is more difficult to visit than other destinations. This perception creates a significant disadvantage for the U.S. in its efforts to compete for world travelers. Our national strategy must include an entry process that is faster, friendlier, and more efficient.
2. **Ask people to visit us, with a nationally-coordinated marketing program.** The U.S. is one of the few industrialized countries in the world today without a nationally-coordinated program designed to promote its destinations to international travelers. Clearly, the U.S. must implement its own nationally-coordinated marketing campaign in order to be competitive with other countries in the new world market.
3. **Demonstrate the value of travel and tourism.** An effective strategy must be an informed strategy, and it is therefore important to invest in assessing and re-assessing both the industry's competitiveness within the world market, and the success of U.S. investments in promotion and ease of travel.

II. STRATEGIC RECOMMENDATIONS

Make It Easier for People to Visit Us: A Report of the Ease of Travel and Public Diplomacy Subcommittee

Situation Analysis

In response to the September 11 terrorist attacks, the U.S. government and the travel and tourism industry have made massive investments in securing borders, facilities and infrastructure. The industry is proud of its partnership with the government in these efforts. However, the many steps the government has taken to exclude potential terrorists, while supported by the travel and tourism industry, regrettably may have created the impression that the United States does not welcome international visitors. In the process of focusing exclusively on security, the U.S. has become less competitive than other countries because the perception has been created that it is more difficult and more costly to travel to the U.S. than elsewhere. The collective expertise of the industry and surveys show that many legitimate potential international visitors now deliberately avoid travel to the U.S. due to real and perceived barriers to entry. U.S. businesses often find it difficult to bring and attract people to the U.S. for training, meetings, conferences and other business activities.[18]

A survey of international travel professionals showed that 77 percent believed that the United States was more difficult to visit than other destinations

While the U.S. has focused on the necessary work of border security with minimal consideration to facilitation matters, other countries have invested in competing for the international traveler, both through direct advertising and promotions[19] and through coordinated government policies aimed at attracting investment in tourism and travelers themselves. These policies include offering visas without charge or permitting visa-free travel[20] as well as coordinating government and private sector actions in order to attract international visitors.

The Department of Commerce's Travel Barometer reports, which survey international travel professionals, support our concerns about U.S. government procedures and insufficient communications as barriers to inbound travel. The recent UK Barometer notes that:

> Starting in 2004, entrance procedure to the U.S. consistently has registered as the top barrier for travel. These barriers included the following factors: misinformation for consumers on entry and exit requirements to the USA, actual entrance procedures to visit the USA, visa processing time. Two-in-three program participants consider misinformation for consumers on entry and exit requirements as a travel barrier.[21]

The Barometer reports from Germany and Mexico echo the themes of difficult entry procedures and poor communications as barriers.

A June 2006 survey completed by1 55 international travel professionals throughout the world showed that 60 percent reported clients were concerned or confused about rules and procedures regarding international travel to the U.S. A separate survey question showed that 77 percent believed that the U.S. was more difficult to visit than other destinations, while only six percent found it easier and 18 percent said "about the same." Respondents repeatedly cited visa requirements, "hassle," price, and the perception that the U.S. was unwelcoming as the reasons that customers chose destinations in other countries.[22]

The following recommendations are designed to address current gaps and deficiencies in U.S. competitiveness in ease of travel, and help restore the U.S. as the world's premier international travel destination.

    I.   Remove Unnecessary Barriers to Travel
    II. Create a Welcoming First Impression
    III. Provide Stronger Voice for Travel and Tourism in Government
    IV. Avoid Inappropriate Taxes, Fees and Regulations

I. Remove Unnecessary Barriers to Travel

These suggestions are intended to ensure that the U.S. reduces barriers to inbound travel, effectively communicates with the prospective visitor and reduce taxes, fees and regulations that target travel and tourism. A successful effort promises to contribute to the image of the U.S. abroad and to the U.S. economy across many sectors. Each subcategory identifies an area in which the U.S. is currently not as competitive as other countries in facilitating legitimate inbound international visitors and provides recommendations to help redress this imbalance.

    1. **Reduce Disruption Threatened by Implementation of the Western Hemisphere Travel Initiative (WHTI).** The WHTI is meant to improve the security of U.S. borders by adopting consistent standards for identity documents. It imposes new requirements for national identity documents on citizens of Western Hemisphere countries, and also applies to U.S. citizens re-entering the U.S.. Unfortunately, relatively short deadlines and failure to communicate with the traveling public has put WHTI in a position to disrupt vital trans-border travel. Travel and tourism will also be greatly affected in states far from the physical border: Florida, California and Nevada have the largest inbound markets for Canadians in terms of spending. A recent survey showed that half of Canadians would go to the U.S. less often or not at all if required to present a passport or other identification at the border.[23] The TTAB therefore urges the Secretary to play a role in reducing the disruption by seeking the following actions:

        • Extend the WHTI deadline by at least 18 months until proven technology standards are agreed upon and implemented and a uniform low-cost alternative to passports are ready for use by all travelers whether by land or sea. As of June 30, 2006 the Senate Appropriations Committee had approved an amendment that would delay implementation of the WHTI until June 1, 2009. We urge the Secretary to support this amendment.

- Make the alternative to the U.S. passport (known as "PASS") under consideration for land border use also available to air and sea travelers.
- As the requirements affecting land borders threaten extensive travel disruptions along the Canadian land border, we strongly recommend that the U.S. government immediately begin to work in partnership with Canadian officials to ensure that travelers on both sides of the border are educated about WHTI requirements and have the proper documentation by the deadline.
- Work with the U.S. Departments of State and Homeland Security to develop and execute a massive communications campaign, in partnership with the private sector, to get the message out about the new requirements.
-

2. **Facilitate Issuance of Non-immigrant (Visitor) Visas (NIVs) to Legitimate Travelers.** The cost and inconvenience of applying for a U.S. visa is clearly a barrier to inbound travel. Many other countries that compete for visitors have no visa requirements or, as in the case of Australia, have a very quick and efficient method for issuing travel authorization. Inbound travel by foreign residents is a U.S. export; the fact that the U.S. is not competitive in the non-immigrant visa function is therefore a self-imposed trade barrier.[24] The travel and tourism industry and the U.S. economy lose when prospective visitors decide not to visit the U.S. due to lengthy waits for visa interviews, prohibitive costs and the sometimes extreme distances visa applicants must travel, causing inordinate additional trip costs just to visit the U.S.

Visa Staffing and Waits: the Current Competitive Situation. The U.S. Department of State, its Visa Office in Washington D.C. and Consular Officers throughout the world have performed a remarkable job in recent years in implementing a host of new security requirements, including the near-100 percent interview requirement for NIV applicants and the requirement to obtain a fingerprint impression from such applicants. The addition of over 500 officers in NIV sections outside of the U.S. is a welcome step forward.

Despite this progress, the NIV function remains chronically understaffed and underfunded relative to the critical role it plays at the frontline of the U.S. public image abroad and to facilitating inbound travel to the U.S. A recent U.S. Government Accountability Office (GAO) report notes that almost half of State's 211 visa-issuing posts reported maximum wait times for visa interviews of 30 or more days and that interview waits were 30 plus days every month at 20 posts. In the same report the GAO reiterated its 2002 and 2005 recommendations that State reassess and prepare a plan to address consular staffing requirements.

We draw attention in particular to the long waits required to obtain a visa interview in Brazil,[25] China, India, Mexico and Venezuela as continuing serious impediments to international inbound travel and tourism. Permanent rationing of access to visas is contrary to facilitating inbound travel and tourism and to public diplomacy goals.

Improve Overseas Visa Facilities. Funding for expanding and improving visa facilities or constructing new facilities overseas is virtually nonexistent. [26] Advertising and promotion cannot overcome the negative publicity the U.S. receives daily in countries where waits for visa interviews are long and facilities are cramped and uncomfortable for prospective visitors and consular staff. We therefore urge greater funding for expanding, improving and opening new NIV facilities and have tentatively identified China, Brazil and India as those countries in particular need of new NIV facilities. We also suggest that the Department of State consider whether existing facilities not currently used for visa issuance could be adapted for that function.

Ensure Effective Program Management for the $700 Million Plus Visa Function. We highlight that visa fees (known as machine readable visa fees) generate significant revenues for the U.S. government and the Department of State. Using State's own figures for annual NIV applications of about 7 million multiplied by the $100 machine-readable visa (MRV) application fee (and excluding all other visa-related fees), MRV fees alone generate $700 million annually, or well over half of State's FY 2007 budget of $1.14 billion for the whole of the Border Security Program. While State retains only a portion of visa revenues, the size, revenue and importance of the visa function demands greater investment in technology, coordination among government agencies and experienced managerial oversight.

The Industry's Offer. The travel and tourism industry is ready to partner with the Departments of State and Homeland Security to improve the visa application process and the arrivals experience in a manner that does not compromise security. Through the Travel Business Roundtable and the TIA, the travel industry is also prepared to assist in highlighting the importance of the travel industry to the U.S. economy and providing or designing supplementary customer service training for consular officers and border agents if so desired. We welcome the opening of new Business Visa Centers and the new emphasis on expediting issuance of B-1 (business) visas. Innovations promised in the Rice-Chertoff Joint Vision (RCJV), such as electronic NIV applications and the planned pilot program for remote NIV interviews through video link, are all steps toward making the process more technologically advanced and therefore less burdensome.

Specific Recommendations Regarding Visitor Visa Policies. We recommend that the Secretary of Commerce seek ways to suggest that the Department of State consider:

- Expanded training for consular officers regarding the importance of travel facilitation and making customer service a part of consular officers' review process;
- Finding ways to quickly reduce consular delays by using technology and more appropriately allocating staff across shifts, working hours, and peak demand seasons;
- Establishing benchmarks for visa wait times, focusing on the delay in obtaining an interview;
- Expanding Business Visa Centers to all 211 visa processing posts worldwide;
- Eliminating the archaic "I" journalist visa designation;[27]
- Creating a communications campaign highlighting the openness of the U.S. and ensuring that senior State officials include this message in their public presentations;
- Re-negotiating visa reciprocity schedules, which unnecessarily limit the duration of visas that the U.S. offers;
- If permitted, reestablish a program that allows those working in the U.S. to renew NIVs without leaving the U.S. in order to reduce the burden on consular resources and improve service to legitimate visa applicants;

- Exploring with Congress whether the personal interview requirement could be waived in appropriate, low risk cases, perhaps with fingerprint capture at the Port of Entry or a remote location;
- Actively seeking a way to eliminate the personal interview requirement for those who have previously provided a biometric indicator and have consistently visited the U.S.; and
- Implementing in all NIV sections the best practices currently in place in certain sections, including:
  - Establishing a "Business Window" at posts, and setting aside time- blocks for business visas
  - Permitting group NIV appointments; and
  - Utilizing business facilitation units.[28]

3. **Maintain and Expand the Visa Waiver Program.** The Visa Waiver Program (VWP) is central to keeping the U.S. competitive for inbound international travel; more than 2/3 of all overseas travelers enter the U.S. under the VWP. Twenty-seven countries' passport holders benefit from the freedom to enter the U.S. without previously applying for short-term visitor visas. New measures to enhance the security of passports themselves, the U.S. VISIT entry-exit system and other processes make visa-free travel to the U.S. more secure than ever. The industry continues to strongly support the VWP and we encourage the U.S. government to expedite entry into the program of every country that qualifies. Further, countries need to know exactly what they need to do to be granted VWP status. VWP applicants are required to achieve a certain set of criteria, yet in some cases, officials from other countries have complained that the U.S. government agencies have not communicated in a clear fashion what these requirements are.

4. **Build on the Success of U.S. VISIT.** We highlight the success of the U.S. VISIT program as an example of effective industry-government cooperation that has enhanced border security with minimal disruption to international visitors. It also acknowledges some remaining challenges, such as full implementation of exit processes and transition from two to ten finger scans and proposed expansion of the program to include additional classes of visitors, including U.S. Lawful Permanent Residents and many Canadian citizens. We look forward to continued public-private sector cooperation to help meet these challenges.

5. **Address Barriers to Air Travel.** Commercial airlines are proud of their investment in technology and procedures to serve security and other government goals. Regrettably, U.S. government agencies have frequently failed to make the investment in technology, customer service and rationalization of forms and procedures to allow that investment to pay off for the industry, the traveler and the U.S. economy. Examples include:

- Absence of sustained agency coordination of domestic and international air passenger prescreening programs;
- Lack of robust data sharing among U.S. government agencies and between the U.S. and other governments, which has led to duplicative and redundant airline passenger data collection and resulting passenger disservice;
- Continued suspension of the Transit Without Visa program, which had facilitated international travel through the U.S. and attracted international service to U.S. airports;
- Threatened massive delays of all international flights to permit CBP to process passenger data provided by airlines (so called "APIS –60");
- Failure to provide funding to airlines for the proposed APIS Quick Query (AQQ) pilot program, which is meant to ensure timely departures of international flights now threatened under the APIS-60 concept;
- Discouraging international carriers from serving U.S. airports by uncompetitive execution of security procedures for flights transiting the U.S.;[29]
- U.S. government agency reluctance to eliminate redundant and outdated paper forms and processes leading to needless inconveniences for arriving passengers. The continued requirement that international visitors complete the paper I-94 form despite the fact that the same biographic information is collected electronically through APIS procedures is one example of this problem.

The list of barriers to air travel and inconveniences faced by air travelers demand that the involved agencies consult with industry, rationalize procedures and fully invest in technology. The Board therefore suggests that the Secretary use his influence to identify these failures as barriers to trade and press the responsible agencies to address them.

II. Create a Welcoming First Impression

While surveys have not been conducted to establish the precise drivers of the recent decline in U.S. reputation, there is evidence to suggest that negative perceptions driven by the real and perceived experience at our borders may play a significant role.[30] Marketing experts understand that the most powerful driver of reputation is word-of- mouth. Any effort to improve the U.S. image in the world must include a thorough assessment of the first impression that visitors form as they enter the U.S., followed by a concerted effort to balance necessary security measures with an equal investment in friendliness and efficiency. Visitors should come away from their first contact with the U.S. feeling that they received a warm welcome.

1. **Staff Federal Inspection Services (FISs) and TSA Fully and Efficiently.** The first contact that many arriving international visitors have with the U.S. is with Federal Inspection Services, most notably Customs and Border Protection (CBP) and the Transportation Security Administration (TSA). There is wide consensus that staffing of at least some FISs and TSA inspection points does not adequately meet demand. Slow entry into the U.S. and delays due to TSA's re-screening stand in stark contrast to efficient procedures in many other countries.[31] Canada and the Netherlands are two examples of countries that have prioritized efficient inspections and air transit services and have succeeded in attracting international air service and passengers disproportionate to their populations.

   Expedite Model Ports of Entry. We emphasize the importance of the Model Ports of Entry (MPOE) element of the Rice-Chertoff Joint Vision (RCJV), which is intended to identify and implement best practices at airports with a large volume of international arriving passengers. United Airlines is involved in the project at Washington Dulles. Full and efficient staffing of FIS facilities in pilot cities, other U.S. ports of entry and U.S. preclearance facilities outside of the country is essential to improving the efficiency and friendliness by which the U.S. processes inbound international travelers.

   Develop Metrics to Evaluate Staffing Patterns. The Model Ports of Entry (MPOE) project should begin by developing appropriate metrics to evaluate staffing and operations at the MPOEs. We also reiterate the offer of industry expertise in staffing patterns to the FISs. Most importantly, we stand ready to work actively with the Secretary to seek full and efficient FIS and TSA staffing at air, sea and land ports.

Leverage Industry Expertise. Members of the Board and other industry participants have already offered their expertise in management of line waits and staffing patterns to the FISs. The TIA has begun discussions with the Under Secretary of State for Public Diplomacy and Public Affairs and remains committed to providing travel industry professionals to assist CBP in developing more flexible queuing strategies. The industry is also waiting for the government's cue to advise FISs on signage and the use of international symbols to direct travelers and prepare them for the inspection process.

Several leading travel companies are willing to loan customer service/hospitality experts who could provide training for CBP officers at the Federal Law Enforcement Training Center in Georgia. Such training could complement CBP officers' vital law enforcement work with training on optimal methods for welcoming visitors to the U.S.

2. **Incorporate Hospitality Within DHS Goals and Performance Review Process.** Many of our recommendations are based on the importance of the efficient functioning of the Department of Homeland Security (DHS). It will be difficult to achieve these goals if DHS does not establish a mechanism within its performance review process that accounts for the needs of the legitimate traveler and the travel and tourism industry in decision-making, goals, resource allocation and employee evaluation.

3. **Better Coordinate Security Requirements with Other Governments.** In recent years, lack of coordination and communication as well as inconsistent standards between the U.S. and other governments have threatened the efficient and free-flow of international travelers into the U.S. and damaged the reputation of the U.S. as a destination. More such threats are on the horizon. A renewed U.S. government commitment to consultation and coordination with other governments, especially regarding security and privacy is critical.

Such coordination between governments facilitates not just international inbound travel, but also international-to-domestic travel and encourages use of the U.S. and its airlines and airports for 3rd country to 3rd country travel. We therefore suggest that the Secretary and his counterparts at DHS, the Department of State and the

Department of Transportation (DOT) direct their staff to actively coordinate activities that affect international travel with their equivalents in other governments.[32] Seeking avenues to eliminate TSA re-screening of international arriving baggage transferred to onward flights is an obvious initial goal.

4. **Provide a Warm Welcome to Arriving International Visitors.** With this goal, the travel industry has offered its services through the Department of State in producing professionally designed "welcome" videos that would play on a loop on flat panel monitors in the international arrivals hall of selected airports. These videos might present welcome messages and instructions, and permit the FISs to deliver timely information to arriving international travelers.

5. **Ensure Accurate and Timely U.S. Government Communications Regarding Travel Requirements.** The plethora of new travel requirements the U.S. has imposed on foreign visitors in recent years has rarely been supported by strong communications from the U.S. government. While the industry continues to be ready to highlight official communications to the traveling public it cannot serve as a substitute for effective direct communications between the U.S. government and the traveling public. As mentioned earlier, Commerce's own Barometer reports underscore the fact that official communications about entry requirements have been substandard and therefore create confusion that discourages travel. The uncertainty created by last-minute decisions and inadequate communications regarding the biometric passport requirement dampened demand for travel and increased negative perceptions of the U.S. We suggest that a true, well-funded communications plan must be an integral part of implementing any new entry or exit requirement, including any expansion of U.S.-VISIT. The industry stands ready to lend its expertise to U.S. agencies in this regard.

III. Provide Stronger Voice for Travel and Tourism in Government

When government officials and agencies speak for security, who in government is charged with speaking for travel and tourism? It is clear that other countries that compete with the U.S. have coordinated visa/entry/exit, air service, regulatory, tax and other policies that favor travel and tourism as well as meaningful budgets for traditional promotional campaigns to attract these visitors. Countries that are competitive for tourism also ordinarily have ministries of tourism or other governmental entities that help coordinate policy decisions that impact this sector. The U.S., by contrast, has no specific Ministry of Tourism or Office high enough to advocate these issues at the highest policy levels in support of this vital, growing sector.

1. **Create an Elevated Voice for Travel and Tourism Within Government**. Since the U.S. Travel and Tourism Administration was dismantled in 1996, the travel and tourism industry has suffered from the absence of a dedicated high- ranking office in the Federal government designed to enhance the industry's role in creating jobs and economic growth. While the Office of Travel and Tourism Industries has served a valuable role in providing research and expertise on the industry, and has served effectively in the international organizations for government policy deliberations and representation, a dedicated higher-ranking office with the power to coordinate government policy to enhance the nation's competitive standing in the global travel market is sorely needed. This office should be designed to accomplish the following:
   - Serve as an institutional home and voice for the industry;
   - Energize the interagency process regarding travel and tourism through an elevated Tourism Policy Council with ex-officio status for private sector representation. All government decisions that potentially affect this industry should receive early attention in the interagency process;
   - Identify existing private sector advisory committees, ensure that they include the right representatives from the industry and see that their recommendations are widely shared across agencies and with other private sector groups and the public; and
   - Coordinate the roles of other government agencies to more effectively expand travel and tourism promotion, product development and infrastructure needs and development.

   Ideally, this office would help to coordinate the implementation of many of the recommendations contained in this paper.

2. **Enhance Coordination Between Federal Agencies, Local Government and Private Sector.** We commend the Secretary for his steadfast dedication to elevating the role of travel and tourism within the Bush Administration. While his leadership is central and critical to advancing our policy goals, the recommendations within this document reflect the diversity of our industry issues and their diffuseness among many Cabinet Departments. Many of these issues

fall outside of the Commerce Department's jurisdiction, including at least some elements of visa policy, public diplomacy, immigration reform, transportation policy and homeland security concerns. In addition, America's mayors and governors have long been on the cutting edge of creative travel and tourism policy. We believe that close coordination among Cabinet Departments with the nation's mayors, governors and private sector interests are all necessary if our industry is to receive the policy consideration it deserves. The successful implementation of the Board's policy recommendations are predicated upon the ability of the federal government to functionally process and execute them.

3. **Create a Private Sector Stakeholders Committee on Visa Matters.** We second the U.S. Chamber of Commerce's recommendation to create an advisory committee of private sector stakeholders that would advise the Departments of State and Homeland Security on visa matters. This suggested committee would be intended to develop cooperative solutions to the visa matters that are key barriers to travel.[33]

4. **Identify Causes Behind Shifts in Travel Away from the U.S.** We suggest that the Department of Commerce identify key countries where international travel has shifted away from the U.S., and determine the causes behind these shifts in travel. Identifying and quantifying travel diversion is the first step towards regaining market share, either through reducing barriers to U.S. exports of travel services or though other means.[34] We welcome the insights available in the Barometer reports and in the Department's recent survey of Foreign Commercial Service (FCS) employees abroad about barriers to inbound travel[35] and we expect that these reports are circulated to State and DHS to inform their efforts.

5. **Fund, Staff and Establish Goals and Metrics for the Rice-Chertoff Joint Vision.** We welcome the intentions of Rice-Chertoff Joint Vision (RCJV), which Secretaries Rice and Chertoff announced in early 2006. The RCJV's goals of easing travel barriers to the U.S. and of improving the U.S. image abroad are congruent with the travel industry's goals, and many of our recommendations could be implemented through the RCJV.

U.S. Departments of State and Homeland Security officials responsible for the initiative briefed Subcommittee staff on progress in the project's first five months. During this period the RCJV seems not to have established concrete goals beyond the normal plans of the agencies nor is it clear that it has any timelines or metrics by which to judge its success. Further, the RCJV has no permanent staff and does not have its own budget. We strongly recommend that Secretaries Rice and Chertoff move quickly to seek the private sector's input in establishing concrete goals, timelines and associated budgets needed to reach those objectives

IV. Avoid Inappropriate Taxes, Fees and Regulations

Federal, state, local, special entity and foreign-government imposed taxes and fees on rental cars, commercial aviation, hotels and restaurant meals, among other services increase the cost of travel and can dampen demand for inbound travel. Much of this tax burden placed on travelers is used to fund programs may be of general public benefit – but have no clear connection or benefit to the industry or consumers being taxed. Government programs that benefit the public at large should not be funded by travel- specific taxes and fees; any taxes and fees directed at travel and tourism should have a clear connection to and benefit those paying the taxes.

In the case of rental cars, special excise taxes fund 18 sports and venue projects and additional such taxes are under consideration. Despite the billions of dollars paid by rental car companies and customers in excess of normal sales taxes there is no special benefit to rental car customers from such special venue taxes nor is there a direct connection between renting a car and using the public facilities or programs the taxes fund. In the case of commercial air transportation, international passengers pay eight types of taxes and fees to the U.S. government in addition to sales taxes, including fees that subsidize security, which is properly a national priority. Air and rental car transportation is not a luxury that should be taxed as such. The fact that other modes of transportation, such as bus and rail are not similarly taxed illustrates this fact. Hotel and restaurant taxes and taxes and fees directed at other aspects of the travel and tourism industry are sometimes similarly overused to fund programs that should be general obligations.

1. **Discourage Inappropriate Taxes and Fees.** In light of the misuse of taxes and fees on travel and tourism at all levels of government, we emphasize that some existing types of taxes for the broad public benefit inappropriately target travel and tourism, thus decreasing the international competitiveness of the U.S. as a destination. We urge the Department of Commerce to work on ways to discourage such discriminatory taxing structures and ask that the Department of Commerce work in the interagency process to discourage travel taxes imposed by international authorities when the revenue raised has no clear benefit or connection to the travel and tourism industry. We also suggest a Commerce study of taxes and fees related to travel across countries in order to help determine the U.S. competitive position in this regard.

2. **Review CBP Rates.** We seek the assistance of the Department of Commerce in reiterating the airline industry's call for a thorough review of CBP rates and charges based on costs.[36] Any further increase in government fees on arriving international passengers directly threatens the goal of attracting international visitors to the U.S.

3. **Head Off Regulatory and Indirect Barriers to Travel.** In addition to direct taxes and fees, mandates from government agencies that target travel and tourism can hamper the goal of facilitating inbound travel. As an illustration, the U.S. Centers for Disease Control's (CDC) recent Notice of Proposed Rulemaking would require cruise lines and airlines to collect massive new amounts of personal data from passengers at a direct cost of up to $800 million annually. No other country imposes the cost of public health directly on the travel industry. As another recent example this year the Department of Transportation proposed to require airlines to provide oxygen free of cost to any passenger upon request, regardless of demonstrated medical need. Complying with this rule, if made final, would raise costs to airlines, dampen demand and possibly make some air service uneconomical. In these and similar matters, we urge the Secretary of Commerce to actively engage in the interagency process with a view to protecting the travel and tourism industries from these and other regulatory threats.

Ask People to Visit Us: A Report of the Promotion Subcommittee

Situation Analysis

The United States is one of the only industrialized countries in the world today that lacks a nationally-coordinated program designed to attract a greater percentage of world travel. Canada, for instance, invests $80 million per year on its national marketing program, and Australia invests more than $100 million. Even New Zealand, a country 1/74th the size of the U.S., invests $43 million each year promoting itself to world travelers.

The absence of a nationally-coordinated campaign that communicates the common qualities of U.S. destinations represents a significant competitive disadvantage.

Other countries use nationally-coordinated programs to formulate consistent, compelling messages with proper timing to ensure maximum effectiveness.

While some individual destinations and private sector businesses from the U.S. currently invest in marketing internationally, the absence of a nationally-coordinated umbrella campaign that communicates the common qualities of these destinations represents a significant competitive disadvantage for the U.S.

The potential rewards of implementing such a campaign are manifold:

- **Provide a Coordinated Message that Communicates the American Experience:** The power of a unifying organizing principle to better leverage the commonalities of individual brands is a proven axiom of marketing – one that is employed by many of the companies represented on this board. Although a number of individual brands and destinations in the U.S. have the resources to market themselves abroad, these efforts are uncoordinated, conflicting, and fail to communicate the deepest, most universal qualities of the U.S. as a brand. An over-arching, umbrella message is therefore necessary to move the U.S. higher on the list of dream destinations.
- **Benefit all Regions Equally:** A nationally-coordinated campaign will help drive visitation higher in those states and regions that cannot afford to market themselves individually. From the neon glow of

Vegas, to the tranquility of the Pacific Northwest, to the music and flavor of the South, to the simple beauty of the plains, to the majesty of the Rocky Mountains, the U.S. tourist experience can be as varied as the imagination, and as affordable or extravagant as one can afford. But unfortunately, without a nationally coordinated program, the vast majority of business and tourist destinations are unable to reach international markets. These destinations will continue to be at a significant disadvantage until a nationally-coordinated program is implemented that can channel visitor interest to other regions of the U.S. beyond the two coasts.

- **Ensure that the U.S. is Top-Of-Mind for World Travelers:** By far the greatest disadvantage posed by our lack of a nationally-coordinated marketing campaign is that the U.S. does not have a vehicle to become "top-of-mind" for travelers as they begin to consider their next vacation or trip. Marketing experts break down the travel planning cycle into separate phases:

  1. *Consideration:* This phase is all about answering the basic question -- "Where should we go?" Targeting potential visitors with the right mass media, in whatever form, sparks their awareness of the U.S. as a travel destination. This is exactly where a well-executed destination marketing campaign will pay significant dividends.
  2. *Planning:* At this stage, travelers gather information and narrow down their choices, so the more compelling, entertaining and appealing the information is, the better.
  3. *Booking:* At this stage, travelers are ready to buy, so tailored, personalized messages should be on hand to help close the deal.

  If the U.S. isn't top-of-mind with potential visitors at phase #1, then the competition will likely be over by phases #2 and #3. These travelers will -- more often than not -- decide to travel elsewhere.

- **Enhance Our National Image:** The image of the U.S. is at an all-time low in many parts of the world – at a time when U.S. reputation matters more than ever. Dollar for dollar, investing in a nationally-coordinated destination marketing campaign is perhaps the most effective vehicle to strengthen the U.S. image in other parts of the world.

1. **Demonstrate that our Doors are Open and the Welcome Mat is out.** Actions speak louder than words, and the simple act of asking people to visit communicates a powerful message in and of itself – even to those who are not able to accept the invitation. We look forward to the day that people around the world receive such an invitation from the United States.

2. **Bring Potentially Millions of Additional Visitors to the U.S.** Whether tied to a company or a country, positive word-of-mouth is the most powerful form of marketing. Research conducted in six of the top travel markets to the U.S. – Brazil, Canada, France, Germany, Japan and the UK – established that while 38 percent of those who had never visited the U.S. had a positive image of the U.S., 54 percent of those who had visited viewed the U.S. positively. Likewise, only 61 percent of those who had not visited the U.S. had a positive view of the American people, compared to 72 percent of those who had visited.[37] By giving these visitors a powerful first-hand experience of our values and hospitality, we can create millions of grassroots ambassadors.

3. **Communicate America's Story to the World Through a Well-Executed Marketing Campaign.** The best marketing campaigns contribute to building a long-term brand in addition to selling a product. Many other countries are doing this very effectively, with destination marketing that communicates the values and culture that define them. The U.S. should be in the international marketplace with similar ads that invite the world to experience the land of life, liberty and the pursuit of happiness.

Recommendations of the Promotion Subcommittee

In order to be fully competitive in the world marketplace, the U.S. must implement a nationally coordinated and properly-executed destination marketing campaign. Without such a campaign, the U.S. will remain at a competitive disadvantage in the market for international travelers.

How to best implement such a campaign is a difficult question – one that has challenged both the industry and many in government for years. Resolving this question will require a more extensive period of time, and the input of the entire travel and tourism industry, as well as other stakeholders in government and the private sector.

It is good news that a new effort is underway, called the Discover America Partnership, to do exactly that. This effort led by prominent players throughout the travel and tourism industry is expected to culminate by the beginning of 2007.

In the interim, we are pleased to offer the following recommendations, based upon industry best practices and successful models implemented by states as well as other countries.

1. **Develop a Viable Framework:** Efforts to launch a nationally-coordinated destination marketing campaign have failed in the past partly due to the absence of a viable framework at the front end. We are pleased to see the private sector take the initiative to develop a comprehensive plan via the Discover America Partnership. This Partnership will use the best marketing expertise of the industry, as well as best practices of other nationally coordinated efforts. The framework should contain the elements listed below:

2. **Determine Funding Requirements**: Determine the level of funding necessary to achieve "share of voice" in the top source markets to the U.S. This recommended funding level should be determined through a rigorous market analysis, looking at current spending by competitor destinations, various communications channels, and other features specific to our target markets.

3. **Identify Viable Funding Sources**: A major factor in the failure of past efforts to create a national marketing campaign has been the lack of a viable, long-term funding model. The high return on investment in terms of jobs, tax revenue, and public diplomacy argue for a significant investment by the federal government in promoting the U.S. to international travelers. However, recognizing the historical challenge of obtaining this money through the congressional appropriations process – coupled with the fact that an appropriation may always be reduced or taken away in any given year – we recommend that the government and the industry also explore other approaches to obtaining funding. The industry should take the initiative in this process by canvassing *all* potential sources of funding, both public and private, and also inventory the successful

funding models used by other countries as well as states in the U.S., as a precursor to building a consensus behind the most viable funding mechanism(s) for this effort. We note that in order to build credibility in asking the federal government to partner in this program, the industry should be willing to contribute at least a portion of the funding.

4. **Identify Target Markets:** The framework should identify the top foreign markets of focus based on data gleaned from the situation analysis. In addition to today's top source markets, our target markets should also include emerging markets – particularly in Asia and Eastern Europe – that are likely to rise rapidly over the next 15 years.

5. **Communicate the American Experience:** The framework should identify the most compelling marketing messages, capturing the diverse alternatives available to tourists in the U.S.

6. **Centralize Resources of Federal Government Agencies:** The Federal government can more effectively focus the Tourism Policy Council to bolster more coordinated and centralized promotional activities among member agencies with the private sector, such as the Department of Transportation's Scenic Byways, the Department of Interior's Parks Services and Fish and Wildlife, the Department of Agriculture's Forest Services, and the Advisory Council on Historic Preservation, to name a few.

7. **Integrate both Public and Private Expertise:** The most successful models in other countries rely on a full partnership between government and the private sector. The private sector typically takes the lead on designing and executing the marketing campaign, including messaging, timing and media channels. However, we note that there are also roles that the government is uniquely suited to help fulfill:
   - *Marshal Resources of Private Sector:* The federal government can act as a galvanizing force to marshal the resources of the private sector travel and tourism industry.
   - *Ensure Program Benefits Entire U.S:* The federal government is in a unique position to ensure that a nationally coordinated destination marketing program is one that benefits tourist

destinations throughout the U.S. – rather than select destinations on the two coasts.

- *Publicize Travel Requirements:* The government should also play a key role in helping to publicize issues that cut across different agencies, so that marketing efforts are not marred by confusion and misinformation. For instance, the communication of changes in documentation requirements would require coordination between the Departments of State, Homeland Security and Commerce.
- *Open Doors in Foreign Markets:* With its extensive network of consulates, embassies and trade offices, the federal government can help open doors in foreign markets, and contribute on-the-ground resources to supplement communications efforts.

Demonstrate the Value of Travel and Tourism : A Report of the Return on Investment Subcommittee

Situation Analysis

Given the stature of travel and tourism as one of the world's most significant growth industries, it is important that the U.S. have processes in place to measure the success of efforts to compete in this market, in terms of job creation, economic impact, tax revenue and U.S. reputation. The ability to measure these returns on investment is particularly important in order to continue to calibrate a national strategy by calculating return on investment and tracking shifts in the marketplace.

The primary data set for measuring the economic impacts of travel and tourism is published by the Bureau of Economic Analysis (BEA) in its Travel and Tourism Satellite Accounts (TTSA). The data set provides standardized measurements of key economic contributions of travel and tourism (T&T) which can be tracked over time. The BEA satellite accounts, as official government statistical reports, have the additional benefit of being accepted by government agencies and the U.S. Congress.

Summary of the U.S. TTSA from BEA

Based on the information provided by BEA,[38] the U.S. TTSA includes estimates of the following variables:

- Output (or Supply)
- Employment (Jobs)
- Value Added (GDP)

Output and Employment

For output and employment, both direct T&T impact and total (including both direct and indirect) T&T impact are provided. The direct tourism output is defined as the value of goods and services sold directly to visitors. The indirect tourism output relates to the production of the inputs used for the direct output.

As shown in Table 1, according to BEA, the U.S. direct tourism output reached about $520 billion in 2003, which accounted for about 2.6 percent of U.S. total output. The direct tourism output increased about 9 percent in 2004 to $566 billion and 8 percent in 2005 to $611 billion. The U.S. total tourism-related output reached about $906 billion in 2003, contributing to 4.6 percent of U.S. total output. The total tourism output also increased about 9 percent in 2004 to $987 billion and 8 percent in 2005 to $1,066 billion.

In 2003, according to the BEA, the U.S. direct tourism employment reached about 5.4 million and accounted for 3.9 percent of U.S. total employment. The direct tourism employment increased about 1 percent to about 5.5 million in 2004. The U.S. total tourism-related employment reached more than 7.9 million in 2003, accounted for 5.8 percent of U.S. total employment and increased about 1 percent to about 8 million jobs in 2004.

However, it is worth noting that the these numbers differ significantly from those produced by the widely cited Travel Economic Impact Model, used by the Travel Industry Association, which measures 7.3 million direct travel-generated jobs, and close to 16 million total travel-generated jobs.

Value Added

In 2003, the U.S. tourism value added was $285 billion based on the BEA approach, which accounted for about 2.6 percent of total U.S. value added.

Table 1. U.S. TTSA Prepared by BEA

Economic Variables	Units	2003	2004	2005
Output (Supply)				
Total Output	$Billion	19,716		
Direct Tourism Output	$Billion	520	566	611
Share in Total Output	%	2.6		
Total Tourism-Related Output	$Billion	906	987	1,066
Share in Total Output	%	4.6		
Employment (Jobs)				
Total Employment	Thousand	137,520		
Direct Tourism Employment	Thousand	5,416	5,486	
Share in Total Employment	%	3.9		
Total Tourism-Related Employment	Thousand	7,909	8,010	
Share in Total Employment	%	5.8		
Value Added (GDP)				
Total Value Added	$Billion	11,004		
Tourism Value Added	$Billion	285		
Share in Total GDP	%	2.6		

Source: BEA

Output and Value Added by Industry

The TTSA provided by BEA analyzed the U.S. economy in terms of 26 industries. The industry level tourism output (tourism value added) was estimated by multiplying the industry level total output (total value added) by the tourism ratio (estimated by BEA) of the corresponding industry. As shown in Table 2, the five industries with the highest tourism ratios in the U.S. in 2003 were: scenic and sightseeing transportation (0.97), intercity bus services (0.95), travel arrangement and reservation (0.93), intercity charter bus services (0.82), and air transportation services (0.79).

Table 2. U.S. Output and Value Added by Industry, 2003 ($million)

Industry	Output		Value Added		Tourism Ratio
	Total	Tourism	Total	Tourism	
Traveler accommodations	130,236	95,958	92,677	68,284	0.74
Food and beverage services	413,976	77,548	196,642	36,836	0.19
Air transportation services	109,002	86,512	63,035	50,029	0.79
Rail transportation services	48,320	1,983	28,606	1,174	0.04
Water transportation services	36,352	6,379	14,297	2,509	0.18
Intercity bus services	1,534	1,454	929	881	0.95
Intercity charter bus services	970	792	800	653	0.82
Local bus and other transportation	21,903	2,838	7,656	992	0.13
Taxicab services	11,013	3,449	7,583	2,375	0.31
Scenic and sightseeing transportation	2,303	2,240	1,704	1,657	0.97
Aotomotive equipment rental and leasing	37,220	21,597	12,953	7,516	0.58
Automotive repair services	107,524	5,968	52,589	2,919	0.06
Parking	10,426	1,640	5,194	817	0.16
Highway tolls	7,781	511	5,958	391	0.07
Travel arrangement and reservation	34,491	32,020	18,514	17,188	0.93
Motion pictures and performing arts	43,013	7,246	17,060	2,874	0.17
Spectator sports	33,104	8,956	23,129	6,257	0.27
Participant sports	41,340	11,090	22,474	6,029	0.27
Gambling	39,991	15,749	22,898	9,018	0.39
All other recreation and entertainment	44,692	12,098	27,185	7,359	0.27
Petroleum refineries	219,524	11,833	31,599	1,703	0.05
Iindustries p roducing nondurable goods	1,884,037	42,274	738,873	16,579	0.02
Wholesale trade and transportation services	1,157,314	19,710	761,352	12,966	0.02
Gasoline service stations	62,207	4,350	50,773	3,550	0.07
Retail trade, excluding gasoline stations	1,070,331	27,171	719,702	18,270	0.03
All other industries	14,147,608	10,857	8,079,863	6,201	0.00
Total	19,716,212	520,000	11,004,045	285,027	0.03

Source: BEA

Table 3. U.S. Employment by Industry, 2003 (Thousand)

Industry	Employment		Tourism Ratio	% in Direct Tourism
	Total	Direct Tourism		
Traveler accommodations	1,782	1,313	0.74	24.3
Food and beverage services	8,704	1,630	0.19	30.2
Air transportation services	647	514	0.79	9.5
Rail transportation services	215	9	0.04	0.2
Water transportation services	159	28	0.18	0.5
Intercity bus services	26	25	0.95	0.5
Intercity charter bus services	25	20	0.82	0.4
Local bus and other transportation	364	47	0.13	0.9
Taxicab services	147	46	0.31	0.9
Scenic and sightseeing transportation	18	18	0.97	0.3
Automotive equipment rental and leasing	179	104	0.58	1.9
Automotive repair services	890	49	0.06	0.9
Parking	81	13	0.16	0.2
Highway tolls	55	4	0.07	0.1
Travel arrangement and reservation	226	210	0.93	3.9
Motion pictures and performing arts	195	33	0.17	0.6
Spectator sports	210	57	0.27	1.1
Participant sports	786	211	0.27	3.9
Gambling	425	167	0.39	3.1
All other recreation and entertainment	452	122	0.27	2.3
Petroleum refineries	74	4	0.05	0.1
Other industries producing nondurable goods	6,878	154	0.02	2.9
Wholesale trade and transportation services	7,265	124	0.02	2.3
Gasoline service stations	664	46	0.07	0.9
Retail trade, excluding gasoline stations	14,759	375	0.03	6.9
All other industries	92,299	71	0.00	1.3
Total	137,520	5,402	0.03	100.0

Source: BEA (June 2005)

**Table 4. U.S. Total Tourism-Related Employment
by Industry, 2003 (Thousand)**

Industry	Direct Tourism Employment	Employment Multiplier	Total Tourism Employment	% in Total Tourism Employment
Traveler accommodations	1,313	1.23	1,616	20.4
Food and beverage services	1,630	1.34	2,180	27.6
Air transportation services	514	1.81	928	11.7
Rail transportation services	9	1.89	17	0.2
Water transport- tation services	28	3.61	101	1.3
Intercity bus services	25	1.40	35	0.4
Intercity charter bus services	20	1.45	29	0.4
Local bus and other transportation	47	1.45	68	0.9
Taxicab services	46	1.43	66	0.8
Scenic and sightseeing transportation	18	1.39	25	0.3
Automotive equipment rental and leasing	104	2.34	243	3.1
Automotive repair services	49	1.55	76	1.0
Parking	13	2.00	26	0.3
Highway tolls	4	1.50	6	0.1
Travel arrangement and reservation	210	1.53	322	4.1
Motion pictures and performing arts	33	2.15	71	0.9
Spectator sports	57	1.70	97	1.2
Participant sports	211	1.29	272	3.4
Gambling	167	1.43	238	3.0
All other recreation and entertainment	122	1.58	193	2.4
Petroleum refineries	4	3.25	13	0.2

Table 4. (Continued)

Other industries producing nondurable goods	154	2.90	446	5.6
Wholesale trade and transportation services	124	1.56	194	2.5
Gasoline service stations	46	1.22	56	0.7
Retail trade, excluding gasoline stations	375	1.20	449	5.7
All other industries	71	1.96	139	1.8
Total	5,402	1.46	7,907	100.0

Source: BEA (June 2005)

In 2003, the five industries that generated most of the tourism output were: traveler accommodations (18.5%), air transportation services (16.6%), food and beverage services (14.9%), other industries producing nondurable PCE goods (8.1%), and travel arrangement and reservation (6.2%). The same five industries also accounted for most of the tourism value added in 2003.

Direct and Total Tourism Employment by Industry

The TTSA from BEA also includes both direct tourism employment and total tourism- related employment by industry. As shown in Table 3, the top 5 industries with the highest shares in total direct tourism employment were: food and beverage services (30.2%), traveler accommodations (24.3%), air transportation services (9.5%), retail trade, excluding gasoline stations (6.9%), and travel arrangement and reservation (3.9%). Total tourism-related employment by industry is provided in Table 4.

Current Measurements Apart from TTSA

In 2005, the U.S. Department of Commerce funded a promotional program promoting travel to the U.S. from the United Kingdom. As part of the overall program, the Department of Commerce contracted with Longwoods Research to measure the impact of the marketing program.

Individual states and cities also have various marketing accountability measurements in place. Many of these are focused on the domestic travel market; however, some have incorporated programs to estimate the impact of marketing activities in international markets. Hawai'i Tourism Authority,

Nevada Commission on Tourism, Mississippi Development Authority, Louisiana Office of Tourism, San Diego Convention & Visitors Bureau, Greater Philadelphia Tourism Marketing Corporation, and others have marketing research in place which could provide a model for measurement of Federally funded international marketing programs.

The U.S. Department of Commerce Office of Travel and Tourism Industries (OTTI) gathers volumetric and demographic information on inbound visitors to the U.S. through inflight surveys; however, sample sizes are small. Additionally, OTTI obtains a summary of international arrivals to the U.S. by type of travel and residency through analysis of Department of Homeland Security I-94 forms.

The Office of Travel and Tourism Industries also publishes the *Travel Trade Barometer*, based on a qualitative survey (small sample size) designed to collect input from active travel trade professionals selling travel to the U.S. The *Barometer* provides general forecasts of trends and demand 3-6 months out.

Statistics Canada provides results of their International Travel Survey to the Office of Travel and Tourism on a monthly basis to report Canadian travel to the U.S. A compilation and analysis of these data is published annually in *Canadian Travel to the United States.*

Some foreign governments and operators publish data on numbers and characteristics of outbound travelers, including travelers to the U.S. In Japan, for example, such data are published by the government, travel media (*Travel Journal International)*, and JTB Corporation for that market.

Gaps and Deficiencies: What Numbers Are We Missing?

While the TTSA provides accepted, comprehensive data on the economic impact of tourism, there are gaps and deficiencies in using them exclusively as an accountability measure for tourism promotion programs.

- The BEA estimates of employment generated by travel and tourism differ significantly from the information generated by the Travel Economic Impact Model, which is widely used by the travel industry.
- Given the significant size of the economic contributions of tourism, it will take a significant investment in promotion across a range of source markets in order to see the promotional impact of tourism

promotion within the overall TTSA accounts. Without significant tourism promotion spending, it would be necessary to isolate TTSA measurements in those markets where promotional spending occurs (and compare those results to the TTSA measurements in non-promotional markets) in order to gauge the impact of tourism promotion based on the TTSA accounts.

- There is a lag in the reporting of TTSA results which limit the usefulness of the data for marketing applications.
- In addition to travel promotion impacts, travel to the U.S. is strongly influenced by other non-marketing variables, including economic conditions, currency rates, restrictive visa policies, terrorist incidents, political disruptions, and airlift among others.
- While there are some measurements of international attitudes toward the U.S. as a country (such as the Pew Report), there are no existing international measurements of consumer intention to travel to the U.S. or consumer attitudes toward the U.S. as an attractive visitor destination. Such measurements would provide a better indicator of the effectiveness of marketing programs than reliance on visitor arrivals or economic impact alone.

Recommendations

1. **Return on investment of marketing campaigns**
   - The Department of Commerce and/or the Travel and Tourism Advisory Board should complete a review of existing research models measuring the impact of travel promotions. These should include previous USDOC measurements, the Longwoods research conducted to measure the impact of the United Kingdom promotional campaign in 2005, and existing state or city marketing effectiveness research. We urge the Department of Commerce to review the methods used by other countries in order to leverage best practices in this area.
   - Based upon a review of existing models, the Department of Commerce should solicit proposals from qualified research companies incorporating best existing practices and their own creative recommendations to measure the impact of travel marketing programs. Ideally, when implemented, such research

should include a measurement of promotional areas compared to a control area.

- Funding for future promotional programs should include an allocation for effectiveness research.

2. **Travel and tourism industry's contributions to economy and job creation**

   - The BEA Travel and Tourism Satellite Accounts estimates differ from those produced by the Travel Industry Association of America (TIA) through its Travel Economic Impact Model using a different methodology. TIA has been working closely with the BEA and OTTI to reconcile these differences and to improve our national statistics for the U.S. travel and tourism industry. We support and recommend that this work be continued.

   - Specific metrics within TTSAs should be identified and consistently reported to opinion leaders and stakeholders. Prospective tracking measurements from the TTSA could include:
     - Direct tourism output
     - Total tourism-related output
     - Direct tourism employment
     - Total tourism-related employment
     - Tourism value added GDP
     - Tourism share of total GDP

3. **Perceptions of U.S. among international travelers**

   - With the adoption of recommendation 1 (measuring return on investment for marketing campaigns), it is possible to design research to measure intention to travel and attitudes toward the U.S. as a travel destination. Unlike the Pew Report (which measures overall attitudes about the U.S.) research can be tailored to specifically measure factors related to travel. Specifically:
     - Respondents can be screened so that the sample is composed of potential international travelers (rather than the population at large).
     - With tracking research fielded in multiple markets, shifts in perceptions can be measured both against a base and against a control in order to ascertain the impact of promotional programs.

   - As noted earlier, a review of existing research models from states and other countries, and the solicitation of research proposals through a request for proposals can provide creative input to develop an effective measurement system for travel attitudes and intentions.

4. **Support for permanent funding.**
   - The implementation of a program to measure marketing effectiveness and track a return on investment should be used as an integral support point for permanent, dedicated funding for tourism promotion.

U.S. TTAB Member Roster

Chairman
   Mr. James Rasulo, Chairman, Walt Disney Parks and Resorts

Vice-Chair
   Ms. Marilyn Carlson Nelson, Chairman and CEO, Carlson Companies, Inc.

Board Members
   Mr. Charles Gargano, Chairman and CEO, Empire State Development Corporation
   Ms. Noel Irwin Hentschel, Chairman, Co-Founder and CEO, AmericanTours International
   Mr. Jeremy M. Jacobs, Sr., Chairman and CEO, Delaware North Companies, Inc.
   Mr. Rex D. Johnson, President and CEO, Hawaii Tourism Authority
   Mr. Lawrence K. Katz, President and CEO, Dot's Diner Restaurant Chain
   Mr. Jonathan Linen, Vice Chairman, American Express Company
   Mr. J. W. Marriott, Jr., Chairman and CEO, Marriott International, Inc.
   Mr. Manuel Stamatakis, Chairman of the Board, The Greater Philadelphia Tourism Marketing Corporation
   Mr. Robert S. Taubman, Chairman, President & CEO, The Taubman Centers, Inc.
   Mr. Andrew C. Taylor, Chairman and CEO, Enterprise Rent-A-Car
   Mr. Glenn F. Tilton, Chairman, President, CEO, United Airlines
   Mr. Jonathan M. Tisch, Chairman and CEO, Loews Hotels

Ex-Officio Members
Mr. Mike Fullerton, Deputy Executive Director, Department of Homeland Security **Mr. Tony Edson**, Deputy Assistant Secretary for Visa Services, Department of State

About the Travel and Tourism Advisory Board

The U.S. Travel and Tourism Advisory Board (TTAB) was formed in late 2005 in order to advise U.S. Commerce Secretary Carlos Gutierrez on how to best increase the number of international visitors to the United States and ensure that the share of the country's international receipts continues to grow.

The advisory board is comprised of 14 top industry executives and leaders from across the Unites States. The selected members represent a bipartisan cross-section of the industry. The Board, which reports directly to the Secretary of Commerce, functions as an advisory body, acting within the guidelines set forth by the Federal Advisory Committee Act

At the Board's first meeting in January 2006, Secretary Gutierrez asked the Board to recommend a new national strategy to enhance U.S. competitiveness in the world travel and tourism market. This strategy was to include an assessment of current market trends, the current ability of the U.S. to compete in this market, and a recommended national strategy for the future.

Three subcommittees were formed in order to carry out this work:

Promotion Subcommittee:

This subcommittee is charged with examining the factors critical to a successful implementation of a long term destination marketing program, including necessary funding levels; source of funding; administration; government and private sector involvement; and target markets. This subcommittee also provides advice on the implementation of current government international tourism promotion activities.

Chair: **Andrew Taylor, Enterprise Rent-A-Car**
         Charles Gargano, Empire State Development Corporation
         Robert Taubman, The Taubman Centers, Inc.
         Manny Stamatakis, The Greater Philadelphia Tourism Marketing Corporation
         J.W. Marriott, Marriott International, Inc.
         Jay Rasulo, Walt Disney Parks and Resorts

Ease of Travel and Public Diplomacy Subcommittee

This subcommittee is charged with recommending improvements in government policy to improve ease of travel and enhance the worldwide image of the United States. Issues include providing policy considerations regarding entry/exit procedures for the United States, barriers to air travel, taxation, and government regulations. This subcommittee also is charged with recommending ways that the industry can partner with the State Department on improving the U.S. image around the world.

Chair: **Glenn F. Tilton, United Airlines**
Jeremy Jacobs, Delaware North Companies, Inc.
J.W. Marriott, Marriott International, Inc.
Andrew Taylor, Enterprise Rent-A-Car
Jonathan Tisch, Loews Hotels
Jay Rasulo, Walt Disney Parks and Resorts
Marilyn Carlson-Nelson, Carlson Companies, Inc
Jonathan Linen, American Express Company
Noel Irwin Hentschel, AmericanTours International

Return on Investment

This subcommittee is charged with recommending national standards to measure the impact of the industry on the economy, balance of trade, job creation travel trends, and market segments. The subcommittee will examine the current set of studies and programs performed by DOC and the industry (including travel and tourism satellite accounts and impact studies) and recommend additional forms of measurement as needed.

Chair: **Rex Johnson, Hawaii Tourism Authority**
Manny Stamatakis, The Greater Philadelphia Tourism Marketing Corporation
Jonathan Linen, American Express Company
Larry Katz, Dot's Diner Restaurant Chain

End Notes

[1] The U.N. World Tourism Organization's *Tourism 2020 Vision* forecasts that international arrivals are expected to reach over 1.56 billion by the year 2020. Of these worldwide arrivals in 2020, 1.2 billion will be intraregional and 0.4 billion will be long-haul travelers.
[2] World Travel and Tourism Council *Progress and Priorities 2006*

[3] The U.S. Travel and Tourism Advisory board consists of 14 industry CEOs, and was formed to advise the Secretary of Commerce on national tourism strategy. The full list of members may be found in the appendix.

[4] U.S. Department of Commerce, U.N. World Tourism Organization

[5] U.N. World Tourism Organization *World Tourism Barometer* January 2006.

[6] U.S. Department of Commerce, Office of Travel and Tourism Industries; U.N. World Tourism Organization

[7] U.S. Department of Commerce, Office of Travel and Tourism Industries; U.N. World Tourism Organization. 2004 is the latest year for which worldwide receipts are available.

[8] U.S. Department of Commerce, U.N. World Tourism Organization

[9] Travel Industry Association estimate.

[10] This is due to the fact that the U.S. receives a greater proportion of its visitation from long-haul travelers, who traditionally spend more money than short-haul travelers. On average, international visitors spent just over $1,600 per visitor in the United States, by far the highest level of spending in any country.

[11] U.N. World Tourism Organization. 2004 is the most recent year for which revenue numbers are available.

[12] U.S. Department of Commerce, Office of Travel and Tourism Industries

[13] U.S. Department of Commerce

[14] The Anholt-GMI Nation Brands Index

[15] Travel Industry Association International Travel Survey of 155 international travel buyers, conducted from June 16-June 26, 2006.

[16] Travel Industry Association of America calculation, using Department of Commerce figures.

[17] The Department of State's FY 2007 Budget Request which shows a request of $351 million for public diplomacy and $474 million for educational and cultural exchanges.

[18] The letters of Mr. J.W. Marriott, Jr., Chairman of the President's Export Council of December 6, 2005 and September 29, 2004 to the President discuss this subject at length.

[19] Australia announced in 2005 that it would spend more than $300 million on international tourism promotion over three years, focused on the U.K, Japan, China and India. Singapore has budgeted $190 million over five years for tourism promotion, while Hong Kong's 2005 budget was $64 million over two years, most of which was directed to global publicity and promotion programs (all figures in U.S. dollars). These figures dwarf U.S. federal government expenditures on tourism promotion both in absolute and per- capita terms ($5.00-$9.00 annually per capita for those three countries, compared to about one cent per capita in the United States).

[20] Canada, for example, permits Korean and Mexican citizens visa-free entry and charges $55 for a single-entry visa (vs. $100 for the United States) and allows a family visa rate that is not available in the United States. Australia's electronic travel authorization visa system is automated, generally free and returns a reply almost instantly, while France charges about $45 for a short-term visa.

[21] UK, Germany and Mexico Travel Barometers, May 2006 Update. U.S. Department of Commerce.

[22] Travel Industry Association International Travel Survey. The survey was held from June 16, 2006- June 26, 2006. 155 completed responses were received during that period.

[23] 2006 Survey of 1,500 Canadian citizens by Leger Marketing made available to the press.

[24] A June 2006 survey of 155 international travel professionals by the Travel Industry Association showed that long waits, cost of visas and distance required to apply for visas were visa applicants' major complaints.

[25] A 1998 GAO report shows Brazil has long suffered from visa backlogs. "Tourist Visa Processing Backlogs Persist at U.S. Consulates," GAO March 1998 pp 2.

[26] In FY 2003 and 2004 State obligated just $10.2 million to 79 consular workspace improvement projects at 68 posts. A GAO report found that even these meager funds were used for temporary solutions at locations awaiting new embassy space. United States Government

Accountability Office, "Border Security; Reassessment of Consular Resource Requirements Could Help Address Visa Delays" April 4, 2006. pp 11.

[27] Eliminating the "I" visa category, which requires journalists who could otherwise travel under the visa waiver program to apply for a visa promises to improve the image of the United States among foreign journalists and to minimally reduce workload in visa sections abroad.

[28] Discussed in State Cable 225608 of October 10, 2004.

[29] As just one recent example, Air New Zealand confirmed in April 2006 that it was abandoning Los Angeles as the stopover on its London-Auckland service due to passenger complaints about security checks at Los Angeles airport. It will move that service over Hong Kong in October. (The Telegraph, "Sunshine State Loses its Allure for Britons," April 8, 2006).

[30] Commerce Foreign Commercial Service officers responded to a survey of impediments to travel to the United States of which 4 identified (mis) treatment of visitors as an impediment to inbound travel. The response from Germany noted, "It is perceived that foreign visitors are unwelcome and we have heard complaints about travelers being treated in the same way as criminals (with fingerprinting and digital photos.)" Many commented that the DHS immigration officers were friendlier on their last visit to the U.S." "Travel Impediments as Reported by Foreign Commercial Service Offices of the U.S. Department of Commerce" May 2006.

[31] Air New Zealand confirmed in April 2006 that it was abandoning Los Angeles as the stopover on its London-Auckland service due to passenger complaints about security checks at Los Angeles airport. It will move that service over Hong Kong in October. (The Telegraph, April 8, 2006, "Sunshine State Loses its Allure for Britons.")

[32] The lengthy negotiations between CBP and the European Commission regarding CBP access to airline passenger data (passenger name records, or PNRs) is an example of the type of involved negotiations required to ensure that U.S. government requirements are consistent with international requirements and do not impede international inbound travel.

[33] Statement of the U.S. COC to the House Committee on Government Reform, April 4, 2006.

[34] A 2005 study of South Koreans' international travel patterns by the Korea Visit USA Committee Commerce illustrates that with the advent of stricter in-person visa interview rules and resulting long waits for interviews in recent years, Korean travel has shifted away from the United States to destinations with minimal entry requirements.

[35] 15 Commerce FCS officers responded to this survey of which 4 identified (mis) treatment of visitors as an impediment to inbound travel. The response from Germany noted, "It is perceived that foreign visitors are unwelcome and we have heard complaints about travelers being treated in the same way as criminals (with fingerprinting and digital photos.) Many commented that the DHS immigration officers were friendlier on their last visit to the U.S." "Travel Impediments as Reported by Foreign Commercial Service Offices of the U.S. Department of Commerce." May 2006.

[36] CBP charges each arriving international passenger a user fee that covers CBP inspections costs. This request for review is particularly urgent given CBP's April 2006 proposal to raise inspections fees across the board. The commercial airline industry has long believed that CBP fees levied on commercial passengers are unjustly high and that these fees subsidize other CBP functions.

[37] Global Market Insite Inc. survey 2005

[38] Source: U.S. Travel and Tourism Satellite Accounts for 2001-2004, by Peter Kuhbach and Bradlee A. Herauf, June 2005 and BEA News Release, March 20, 2006.

INDEX

permit, 115, 118
Peru, 63, 66
Philippines, 63, 66
platform, 101
pleasure, vii, 1, 2, 4, 6, 10, 68
Poland, 63, 66
policy levels, 119
policy makers, 82
population density, 34
population growth, 19
Portugal, 64, 67
poverty, 14, 19
primary data, 128
profitability, 22
project, 8, 98, 116, 117, 121
promotion campaigns, 97
prototype, 6
public expenditures, 5
public health, 122
public parks, 15
public support, 22
public-private partnerships, 13

Q

query, 35

R

race, 23
radar, 90
reading, 31
real estate, 19
recession, vii, ix, 1, 3, 7, 17, 21, 23, 82, 89, 96, 100, 101
reciprocity, 113
recommendations, iv, 108, 110, 112, 117, 119, 120, 121, 126, 136
recreation, 6, 19, 27, 29, 31, 34, 79, 131, 132, 134
redevelopment, 20
reforms, 92
relatives, 31
repair, 27, 29, 130, 132, 133
reputation, 107, 116, 117, 124, 128
resource allocation, 117

resources, 12, 114, 123, 127, 128
restaurants, 3, 6, 12, 19, 24
retail, 23, 25, 131
revenue, ix, 15, 18, 19, 22, 26, 33, 78, 87, 91, 96, 100, 102, 103, 104, 105, 106, 113, 122, 126, 128, 141
rewards, 123
rhetoric, 82
rural areas, 13, 19
Russia, 63, 66

S

screening, 116, 118
Secretary of Commerce, 87, 113, 122, 139, 140
Senate, 32, 75, 81, 85, 89, 90, 95, 99, 111
servers, 82
shape, 4
ships, 3, 26, 86, 89
shores, 97
shortage, 20
signals, 93
signs, 23, 24
silver, 93
Singapore, 64, 67, 141
small businesses, 102
social phenomena, 3
South Africa, 64, 67
South Dakota, 23
South Korea, 63, 65, 68, 72, 142
Spain, 28, 63, 65, 68, 101, 105, 106
specific tax, 121
spelling, 3
Spring, 34
staffing, 112, 116, 117
stakeholders, 120, 125, 137
State Department, 107, 140
statistics, 6, 41, 42, 77, 82, 87, 106, 137
stigma, 18
stimulus, ix, 86, 90, 99, 102
surplus, viii, 8, 73, 74, 76, 101, 106
survey, 10, 14, 18, 33, 62, 64, 107, 108, 109, 110, 111, 120, 135, 141, 142
sustainability, 87, 93
sustainable growth, 90